THE
COMPLETE
MONTESSORI
METHOD
BOOK

Nurturing Creativity and Independence
in Babies, Toddlers and Preschoolers

KIM SUZUKI

CONTENTS

INTRODUCTION

Welcome, dear parent, to an extraordinary journey into the captivating world of parenting. This expedition invites you to wholeheartedly embrace the Montessori approach, a time-honored philosophy that has accompanied children and parents for well over a century. Within the pages that follow, we will immerse ourselves in the profound and enchanting principles of Montessori, untangling their magical ability to shape the early years of your child's life. As we navigate these chapters, you'll discover how Montessori fires up your child's imagination and encourages their independence, all while kindling a sense of wonder that will accompany them on their remarkable exploration of the world.

Parenting is a unique and challenging adventure, often described as a journey into the unknown. As we embark on this path, we are filled with hopes, dreams, and a deep desire to provide the best for our children. We yearn to see them flourish, to watch them develop into confident, self-sufficient individuals who are capable of navigating the complexities of the world with grace and resilience. However, this experience can be daunting and overwhelming, especially in a world where there is an abundance of conflicting advice, methods, and philosophies competing for our attention.

The vast array of parenting information available today can often lead to confusion and self-doubt. It's easy to become lost in the sea of advice, not knowing which direction to take or which method to follow. This complexity can make the task of parenting feel like a difficult battle, filled with uncertainties and unpleasant challenges.

This is where the Montessori method shines as a beacon of clarity and simplicity. In the midst of the noise and confusion, Montessori offers a straightforward and holistic approach to parenting. It provides a clear path that aligns with your child's natural inclinations and developmental stages, making the task not only manageable but also deeply rewarding.

Through the simple Montessori guidelines, you will discover that parenting can be a joyful and fulfilling experience. They offer a road map that empowers you to tap into your child's innate potential and guide them toward becoming the capable and independent individual they are meant to be. So, as we embark on this remarkable expedition together, let the Montessori method be your guiding star, showing you the best direction to take.

Discovering the Montessori Method

Our journey into the heart of the Montessori method is a voyage of discovery, one that promises to illuminate the path of parenting with newfound clarity and purpose. At the heart of this undertaking lies a profound purpose: to provide parents with a potent instrument for nurturing creativity and independence in children, from birth to school age, and beyond. As parents, we are acutely aware that parenting defies a one-size-fits-all approach, acknowledging the vast diversity of family dynamics and circumstances that grace our world. It is precisely this recognition that is the driving force behind this book, which is committed to equipping you with the knowledge and tools needed to adapt the Montessori principles to your unique family setting.

The overarching theme that runs throughout this guide is empowerment—empowering you, the parent, to assume the role of a confident and compassionate guardian of your child's development. Montessori is far more than a mere collection of educational techniques; it is a profound yet simple paradigm that instills in you a deep understanding of and reverence for your child's individuality. It extends an invitation to actively engage in your child's adventure of growth and self-discovery. As you embrace the Montessori principles laid out in these chapters, you will uncover the art of curating an environment that not only fuels your child's innate curiosity but also nurtures their burgeoning independence. It is a pathway to kindling a lifelong passion for learning in your child's heart.

The Montessori method is a treasure trove of wisdom that, once unlocked, will empower you to create a home that serves as a haven for your child's exploration and self-expression. It invites you to perceive your child not as a passive recipient of knowledge but as an active participant in their own development. You will learn how to transform your home into a sanctuary where your child's independence is celebrated and their abilities are nurtured. This, dear parent, is the essence of our journey together—to explore, adapt, and apply the profound principles of Montessori to your family's unique circumstances, and watch as your child blossoms into the remarkable individual they are destined to become.

Empowering Parents for a Transformative Journey

I know that parenting can sometimes feel overwhelming. As a parent, you may have come across a lot of advice, which can often be confusing to navigate. But fear not; this book will simplify the Montessori method for you, breaking down its core doctrines into practical, manageable steps that you can integrate into your daily life. The style of this guide is friendly, informative, and simple, designed to make the Montessori philosophy accessible to parents of all backgrounds and all levels of experience.

If you're looking for a simple and effective approach to education, the Montessori philosophy can be your guiding light, offering a holistic and straightforward path to cultivating your child into a confident and capable individual. So, whether you are a first-time parent looking for guidance on how to create a nurturing environment for your newborn, a seasoned caretaker seeking fresh insights into early childhood education, or somewhere in between, this guide is for you.

If you're interested in the Montessori education system, you probably already know that it emphasizes a child's independence, individuality, and natural development. This approach is rooted in the belief that every child has unique potential and that their learning should be tailored to their needs, interests, and abilities. As a Montessori parent, you believe in your child's potential and are eager to support their path of self-exploration. You understand that education is not just about academics, but also about social, emotional, and physical growth. The information in this book is for anyone looking to learn more about Montessori and how it can help their child. Whether you're new to the Montessori community or have been involved for years, there is always something fresh to discover and learn.

In the chapters that follow, we will delve into the essence of the Montessori method, exploring its history, vision, and philosophy, and the practical ways in which you can apply its principles to your daily life. We will discuss the importance of creating a prepared environment that supports your child's development, the role of observation in understanding your child's needs and interests, and the significance of fostering independence from a young age.

Furthermore, we will explore the critical concept of freedom within limits—a cornerstone of Montessori philosophy. You will learn how to strike a balance between allowing your child the freedom to explore and make choices while also providing the fundamental structure and guidance needed to ensure their safety and well-being.

Throughout these pages, I will share real-life stories from parents who have successfully embraced the Montessori method, demonstrating how it has positively impacted their children's lives. These anecdotes serve as a source of inspiration and validation, showing that the Montessori approach is not only a theory but a practical and achievable way of raising children.

Open your heart and mind to the Montessori philosophy and trust in your child's potential and their innate power to discover, develop, and succeed. Montessori is not just another parenting method; it is a proven path to promoting your child's natural abilities and transforming them into competent, autonomous individuals.

So, let's venture forth on this exciting exploration together, with the awareness that the ultimate destination isn't a physical place but a future where your child stands firmly equipped with essential skills, knowledge, and self-assuredness to face life's diverse challenges. Through the method, we are not just nurturing our children; we are planting the seeds of positive transformation in the world they will one day inherit and shape. This commitment represents an investment in the infinite potential of future generations, where the spirit of curiosity, independence, and lifelong learning will illuminate the path toward a better tomorrow.

CHAPTER 1:
MONTESSORI FUNDAMENTALS

In studying the Montessori method we go straight to a very interesting central point: the extraordinary manifestation of the psychic life of the young child. —Maria Montessori

Delving into the core principles of the Montessori method, we find that it is a child-centered educational approach that emphasizes the importance of a supportive learning environment. It encourages children to explore and learn at their own pace, which fosters their creativity, independence, and self-motivation.

The Montessori method teaches that children learn best through hands-on, practical experiences that allow them to explore and discover the world around them. Sensory experiences are important, and children should be encouraged to learn through their senses. Additionally, following their interests and passions helps them to develop a love for learning.

By adopting the Montessori mindset, parents can create an environment that nurtures their child's natural curiosity and creativity. We can provide materials that encourage exploration and self-expression and promote independence by allowing our children to make choices about their learning. Ultimately, the Montessori method empowers children to become self-directed learners capable of achieving their full potential. Throughout this chapter, I have included stories from parents who have successfully implemented the proposed methods in their own homes to illustrate the benefits of the underlying philosophy.

Montessori Philosophy Unveiled

As parents navigating the world of early childhood education, we can find comfort in the enduring principles of Maria Montessori's philosophy. These timeless teachings continue to provide a valuable guide to the development of young children, helping to lay a strong foundation for their future success.

Emergence of a Movement

Maria Montessori, an Italian physician and educator, initially pursued a career in psychiatry during her early days in medicine. However, her interests soon shifted toward education, prompting her to enroll in pedagogy courses and delve into educational theory. This journey led her to question the existing methods employed to teach children with intellectual and developmental disabilities, casting doubt on their efficacy. By 1900, she had taken on the role of co-director at a newly established institute for training special education teachers. Maria approached this task with a scientific mindset, methodically observing and experimenting to pinpoint the most effective teaching techniques. To the surprise of many, numerous children exposed to these methods exhibited remarkable progress, demonstrating the program's success.

In 1907, she faced a new challenge: establishing a full-day childcare center in San Lorenzo, an impoverished inner-city district in Rome. This groundbreaking institution, the first of its kind in the nation, would later become the inaugural *Casa dei Bambini*, providing a high-quality learning environment. Initially, the children displayed unruly behavior, but they quickly became engrossed in activities such as puzzle-solving, learning meal preparation, and engaging with educational materials crafted by Maria herself. She observed how the children naturally absorbed knowledge from their surroundings, essentially becoming self-learners. Drawing on scientific observation and her previous experience with young children, Maria designed learning materials and classroom settings that nurtured the children's innate desire to learn while granting them the freedom to select their own materials.

Contrary to many people's expectations, the children in Maria's programs succeeded, displaying great concentration, attentiveness, and spontaneous self-discipline. The "Montessori Method" began to garner attention from prominent educators, journalists, and public figures. By 1910, Montessori schools had sprouted up across Western Europe and were establishing themselves globally, including in the United States, where the first Montessori school opened its doors in Tarrytown, New York, in 1911.

As of 2023, more than 15,000 Montessori schools have been identified throughout the world. This number is expected to grow, as more and more parents and educational workers realize the power of self-directed learning, and that a curriculum is best tailored around the child's natural interests and focus, and not the other way around.

In our exploration of this philosophy, we'll uncover its unchanging relevance in the modern world and understand its profound impact on our children's growth. Through the real-life narratives shared, we'll witness firsthand the transformative effects of the Montessori method in the lives of parents and children. Maria Montessori's groundbreaking insights continue to resonate, offering invaluable guidance in nurturing young minds and fostering multiple values that characterize the children raised within it. Welcoming these principles not only shapes our children's present but also lays a strong foundation for their future, ensuring they navigate the complexities of life with confidence, curiosity, and a voracious desire to discover new things.

Montessori's Vision of Early Childhood

As noted above, Montessori's method emphasizes on creating an environment that nurtures independence, self-discipline, and a love for learning. She believed that children should be given the freedom to follow their interests and natural curiosity, guided by attentive and supportive adults. This approach not only cultivates academic skills but also nurtures essential life skills such as problem-solving, critical thinking, and empathy.

In this section, we will dive into this vision and explore its practical implications for your child's development. We'll uncover the principles that underpin the method and provide insights into how these principles can be applied in your home. By understanding Montessori's profound insights, you'll be better equipped to create an environment that aligns with the child's natural wiring, setting the stage for a natural and healthy development.

The Sensitive Periods

Central to the Montessori philosophy are the "sensitive periods," a concept that Maria Montessori observed through her extensive work with children. Sensitive periods refer to specific windows of time during a child's development when they are particularly open to certain types of learning experiences. These periods align with critical milestones and represent a child's innate drive to acquire specific skills and knowledge.

Montessori identified several sensitive periods, each with its unique focus and characteristics.

Sensitive Period for Language Acquisition (Birth to Six Years)

The journey of language acquisition begins in infancy and continues throughout a child's early years. During this sensitive period, children display an exceptional receptivity to linguistic development. They rapidly assimilate vocabulary, sentence structure, and the intricacies of language with astonishing speed and precision. Their young minds act as sponges, absorbing words and their meanings from the surrounding environment. This phase is a time of linguistic wonder, where parents and caregivers play a crucial role in nurturing a child's language skills.

Sensitive Period for Order and Precision (Two to Four Years)

Between the ages of two and four years, children undergo a distinctive phase marked by a profound yearning for order and precision in their surroundings. They exhibit an inherent need for consistency and predictability in their daily routines. This sensitive period extends beyond mere tidiness; it represents a deep-seated drive to establish a structured world in which objects have defined places and purposes. Parents can harness this inclination by providing an organized environment that encourages tidiness and meticulousness.

Sensitive Period for Movement and Coordination (Birth to Five Years)

From the moment they begin crawling to their initial steps and beyond, children embark on a hunt to refine their motor skills. This period, spanning birth to five years of age, is characterized by a genuine interest in movement and coordination. It is a time when children enthusiastically explore their physical abilities, from grabbing objects to mastering complex movements. As parents, your role is to furnish a secure and stimulating environment that promotes the advancement of these motor skills, allowing your children to mature into self-assured and coordinated individuals.

Sensitive Period for Sensory Exploration (Birth to Five Years)

For young children, the world is an exquisite realm of sensory experiences, and from birth to five years of age they embark on a charming voyage of sensory exploration. During this sensitive period, children are naturally drawn to tactile, auditory, and visual stimuli that help them understand their environment. Whether they involve experiencing various textures or reveling in the melodic sound of nature, these sensory revelations are the foundation of cognitive development. As parents, you can enrich this exploration by providing an environment with abundant sensory stimuli, encouraging curiosity, and promoting sensory awareness.

Sensitive Period for Social Development (Two to Four Years)

Between the ages of two and four years, children undergo a substantial transformation in their social development. They become increasingly interested in interacting with their peers and cultivating essential social skills. This sensitive period signifies the emergence of empathy, cooperation, and the ability to navigate intricate social interactions. As parents, you have a pivotal role to play in fostering these social skills by offering opportunities for positive social interactions and modeling respectful and empathetic conduct.

The Importance of Comprehending the Sensitive Periods

Understanding these sensitive periods is of essential importance for parents. It allows you to tune in to your child's developmental needs and interests with precision. When you recognize that your child is in a sensitive period for language, for instance, you can provide them with the right tools and opportunities to boost their linguistic skills effectively.

By recognizing when your child is going through a sensitive period, you can offer appropriate learning materials and experiences that support their growth. Throughout this book, you will explore some real-life case studies that illustrate how these sensitive periods affect children's development. This knowledge will help you align your parenting approach with your child's natural inclinations, fostering a more harmonious and productive learning path.

Creating a Montessori Environment

Transforming your home into a Montessori haven is a pivotal step in embracing this philosophy. This section guides you through the process of creating an environment that aligns with the method's principles. We'll address safety considerations and provide tips on setting up age-appropriate spaces to support your child's exploration and independence. Additionally, you'll be inspired by the transformative tales of parents who have successfully undertaken Montessori makeovers in their homes, proving that even small changes can yield significant results.

Kid-Friendly Kitchen Space

An essential aspect to contemplate when crafting your Montessori-inspired home is the kitchen, a hub of daily activities. Elevate your child's independence by establishing a child-friendly space within this culinary area. Create a designated low cabinet or drawer, thoughtfully stocked with children's plates, cups, and safe kitchen tools suitable for your child's age and abilities. When the child is old enough, opt for the learning tower, which puts the child at counter's height, allowing them to observe and participate in daily tasks. It's crucial to be mindful of your child's reach, ensuring that sharp objects like knives and heating devices are securely out of their grasp.

This thoughtfully designed kitchen space will empower your child to actively immerse themselves in meal preparation and cleanup, planting a profound sense of responsibility and capability from the earliest stages of their development. Encouraging their participation in these everyday tasks not only boosts independence but also strengthens their practical life skills. It is within this child-friendly kitchen enclave that your child will begin to embrace the joy of contributing to the family's daily routines, setting a foundation for a lifetime of self-sufficiency.

Let's hear from an anonymous parent about their experience of establishing a specific kid-friendly space in their kitchen:

I was excited to embrace the Montessori philosophy in our home, so I decided to create a space in our kitchen for my son. I emptied a drawer, just at his height, and filled it with children's containers, mugs, and safe tools. It was amazing to see how this simple change allowed my son to participate in cooking and cleanup, giving him a sense of responsibility and capability from a young age. I also identified the drawer clearly with some colourful stickers that he liked and told him several times that this drawer was his, and the other drawers were for mommy and daddy only. After that, I rarely had to tell him not to open the other drawers and cabinets and felt confident enough to remove the child's locks everywhere. It's these small but meaningful adjustments that make me wonder how much more simple could parenting be if we only understood children better.

You can also extend this principle to other areas of your house. Cora shares how she set up a little workspace in her study for her daughter:

I wanted to create a productive workspace for my child to do her crafts activities while I worked from home. So, I transformed a corner of my home office into a kid's studio with a small desk, colorful chair, inspiring artwork, and a whiteboard. This setup made homework feel like a game for her, and she could focus better. Now, she has her own space right next to mine, and it's a win–win for both of us.

The Entryway

The entrance of your home is a great place to promote independance, offering countless opportunities for your child to take on new challenges, one small step at a time. Make sure to have a bench or a nearby staircase, where your child can sit to put on or take off their boots and shoes. An accessible basket containing only the child's belongings such as hats, mittens, scarf, etc. is a must. Also, make sure to have a safe hook at your child's height to allow them to hang their clothes. Finally, have a mirror where they can make sure they have properly dressed before leaving the house.

Learning Towers

A learning tower is an exceptional piece of furniture specially crafted for young children, and it can prove to be incredibly practical. It's ingeniously designed with safety in mind and some models offer adjustable height settings.

What makes this piece truly remarkable is its ability to foster independence in kids. It allows them to stand at counter or table height, facilitating their involvement in various kitchen activities, either collaboratively or autonomously.

Positioning children comfortably alongside adults imparts a sense of equality, encouraging them to imitate their parents' actions. Learning towers serve as an outstanding tool for nurturing confidence, cooperation, autonomy, and a profound sense of contributing actively to family endeavors.

Compared to conventional chairs or stools, these towers provide a much safer and more enriching learning experience for children, offering them valuable opportunities to both learn and have enjoyable moments with their parents. Ultimately, learning towers play an integral role in children's growth and development by enabling them to embrace independence securely within the family dynamic, making them an indispensable hallmark of the Montessori philosophy.

Harold, father of a three-year-old, exemplifies how useful the tower can be:

> Our three-year-old daughter was constantly asking to be held in our arms when we were preparing something in the kitchen. It wasn't out of a need for affection or security, but rather a strong desire to observe and participate in the activities that were going on. With sore arms and a mind that was very open to solutions, my wife and I heard through a friend about the Montessori learning towers. Let me just say that this addition has completely changed the kitchen dynamics. Our three-year-old can now actively participate in meal prep, cooking, even emptying the top of the dishwasher, and we can finally relax our arm muscles!

One day, she confidently grabbed some ice from the freezer all by herself while standing in the tower, then put the tower back against the kitchen island, and went on to put the ice in her glass of juice. It's nothing fancy of course, but the joy I felt watching her grow her independence in this way was something I will never forget. This tower has become an essential part of our daily routine, and we can't imagine our kitchen without it.

Thoughtful Toy Organization

The Montessori method encourages thoughtful toy organization. Instead of overwhelming your child with an abundance of toys, opt for a small shelf where they can see all their toys at a glance. This setup allows your child to choose and play with toys independently, while also promoting responsibility by encouraging them to clean up after themselves. When each toy and object have a clear designated space, it's a lot easier for children to put the object back where it belongs after they are done, Additionally, consider rotating toys periodically to keep their interest piqued and promote extended playtime with each toy.

Adapting Your Child's Room

Your child's bedroom is a vital space for promoting independence. Embrace the idea of the famous floor bed, which allows your child to crawl or walk on and off the bed unassisted, cultivating a sense of autonomy in their sleep routine.

A low bookshelf in their room, plus a comfortable reading spot filled with books of their choice on their favorite topics, creates a reading-friendly environment that encourages literacy from an early age. Keep the bookshelf accessible so your child can pick up a book whenever the mood strikes and enjoy it in a cozy place.

Adding a night-light is a good idea too. Its purpose is to be handy if your kid needs it; otherwise, it should be kept off. Darkness is fundamental for ensuring rest and a good night's sleep. Moreover, including a laundry basket improves your child's sense of responsibility and organization, driving them to keep their space as clean as possible with everything in its place, including the laundry.

What about hanging a mirror in their room? Of course! It should be placed according to your kid's height in order for them to be able to use it and actually see themselves reflected. The aim is not to encourage vanity, but to enable them to check if their clothing and other aspects of their personal presentation are well organized. In addition, you can install some hooks near the mirror; in this way, they can hang their coats or clothing easily.

Sarifa has a three-year-old boy who recently learned how to dress himself. She opted for the mirror inside the room idea and is now telling us about that experience:

As a mother, I decided to add a simple mirror to my three-year-old son's room, thinking it could be a fun addition. Little did I know just how impactful it would be. One morning, as I quietly observed him, I saw something beautiful unfold. He stood in front of the mirror, trying to adjust his shirt just like he'd seen me do countless times. It was a moment of sheer joy and pride as I watched him figure it out on his own. That simple mirror gave me the feeling that my baby was turning into an independent little man. It warmed my heart and made me realize that sometimes, it doesn't take much to empower our children in remarkable ways.

Mindful Decoration

When considering the decor of your child's space, opt for a neutral and calming aesthetic. Avoid excessive use of plastic materials and instead opt for natural materials such as wood, bamboo, glass, and natural fiber materials. A neutral decor not only creates a soothing environment but also allows your child's personal touches and preferences to stand out. It's not necessary to fill the room with colorful wallpaper or bright colors. Instead of having huge cartoon posters or paintings, try using family pictures. Additionally, giving kids the freedom to organize their own room and choose their own style can enhance their independence. You don't have to choose for them thinking they're not old enough to do so; instead, it's important to direct your child while taking into account the Montessori method.

The importance of thoughtful design choices that align with Montessori principles must be emphasized. These changes can be transformative, making your home a space where your child can explore, learn, and thrive independently. Remember, even small changes can yield significant results in nurturing your child's growth and independence.

Montessori Mindset for Parents

As Montessori parents, we believe in empowering our children to become confident, self-sufficient individuals who are capable of making their own decisions. By providing a nurturing environment that fosters exploration and self-discovery, we support our children in developing their innate tendency to learn and achieve tasks on their own terms. Through this approach, we celebrate their successes and help them learn from their mistakes, all while promoting a sense of independence and self-reliance that will serve them well throughout their lives.

Embracing Independence

The Montessori method believes in empowering children to investigate, acquire knowledge, and complete tasks autonomously, recognizing their capabilities are greater than conventional wisdom assumes. You will discover that the approach honors your child's inclinations and capacities. In this section, you'll gain valuable insights into how to create an environment that encourages self-sufficiency, self-discovery, and a lifelong love for learning.

Unlocking Your Child's Capabilities

Children are curious, resilient, and eager to understand the world around them. This method doesn't rush children to grow up; instead, it amplifies their natural abilities, guiding them toward realizing their full potential. By providing opportunities for children to engage in age-appropriate tasks and activities, we nurture their sense of self-efficacy and confidence.

The Joy of Discovery

Children have an inherent drive to explore and understand the world. They want to know how things work, from a new toy to a simple broom. Montessori encourages parents to embrace this curiosity and foster independence by letting children explore and learn at their own pace. Whether it's discovering the purpose of objects, figuring out how things fit together, or simply sweeping the floor, every exploration is a step toward greater understanding and independence.

Note that it's not important that the child figures out immediately how a certain object is meant to be used. If you see them using a spoon to drink their water, or a broom to dust off the coffee table for example, let them explore freely. As long as what they are not putting themselves or anybody else around in danger, and they are not bound to break or damage anything, try observing them without interferring. The simple act of commenting can often put an end to their independant exploration.

Montessori Discipline and Communication

Effective discipline and communication are essential elements of Montessori parenting. We'll delve into both of these aspects, discussing how to approach discipline with respect and understanding. You'll discover strategies that promote cooperation rather than oppression. Additionally, we'll explore the significance of clear and empathetic communication with your child.

Embracing Discipline

Within the Montessori philosophy, infusing discipline involves fostering self-control and responsibility in children. Rather than resorting to punitive actions, we emphasize the importance of setting clear limits and creating a structured environment where children have the freedom to make choices within those defined limits.

It's essential to model respect, kindness, and patience, demonstrating the behavior you want your child to adopt. Consistency and established routines are key to helping children feel secure and understand expectations. Redirecting inappropriate behavior toward more suitable alternatives is another valuable strategy. Moreover, Montessori discipline aims to develop a child's ability to self-regulate, be independent, and show respect for themselves and others, contributing to a harmonious and conducive learning environment:

- **Set clear expectations:** Establish precise and clear guidelines for behavior to help your child understand boundaries.

- **Offer positive reinforcement:** Utilize praise and incentives to motivate and reinforce desirable behavior.

- **Provide gentle guidance:** When necessary, gently guide your child toward more appropriate activities or behaviors.

- **Lead by example:** Exhibit positive behavior as a constructive model for your child to emulate.

- **Promote honest communication:** Cultivate transparent and open dialogue with your child, allowing them to express their opinions and feelings while addressing any questions or concerns they may have.

Empowering Communication Skills

One valuable approach involves enhancing your child's communication skills. You can achieve this by gently encouraging them to repeat what they've just asked or commented on. This simple practice encourages their young minds to slow down, articulate their thoughts once more, and reflect on their words, promoting clearer and more effective communication. Furthermore, exposing your children to other languages or even introducing sign language could be a great idea.

The Power of Respectful Listening

Respectful and active listening form the foundation of effective communication. When children experience respect and attentive listening from their parents, they internalize these values. This new-found understanding then becomes evident in their own communication habits. They begin to grasp the importance of listening to others when they speak, encouraging a culture of respectful conversation. It's worth noting that your actions serve as a powerful model for your child, so maintaining a calm tone and avoiding yelling are essential practices.

Nonverbal Expression

Nonverbal signals, such as smiling, making eye contact, and nodding, play a pivotal role in communication. These subtle gestures convey empathy, understanding, and engagement. When children observe and experience these nonverbal expressions from their parents, they learn to incorporate them into their own communication skills, enriching their ability to connect with others.

Moreover, sign language can be learned from a very young age. This is an interesting option to include in your children's education as it promotes not just their cognitive skills but also inclusion.

Regular Conversation as a Bonding Experience

Frequent and meaningful conversations between parents and children not only strengthen their bond but also boost confidence. Using simple language and clear linguistic structures that match your child's developmental stage ensures that communication is not only meaningful but also comprehensible. When their words make sense and are acknowledged, children are more likely to learn and incorporate effective communication skills into their daily interactions.

Pinilla, father of two boys, talks about the way they solve problems at home:

> *When arguments arise, we encourage each family member to express their thoughts and feelings calmly and respectfully. It's about listening actively, acknowledging each other's perspectives, and finding common ground. This approach not only resolves conflicts more harmoniously but also teaches our children the value of courteous discourse in their own interactions. It's an essential aspect of our Montessori-inspired parenting journey, where we aim to nurture not only independence, but also empathy and respect in our children's lives.*

If your child is still very young and has difficulty expressing their feelings, it can be helpful to ask them simple yes or no questions to try to understand better. Just make sure that the child feels your genuine consideration for them, and that it is completely okay and normal to go through what they are going through at the moment. And finally, reassure them that they have your support no matter what.

The Montessori Journey Ahead

Our next step is to embark on a voyage through the various stages of your child's development, from the early preschool years to the exciting transition into school-age adventures.

But our journey doesn't end with the final page of this book; it's just the beginning. We'll also delve into how to sustain Montessori principles beyond the preschool years, ensuring that your child continues to flourish as they advance along their educational path.

So, engage your creativity and recognize that the Montessori principles are adaptable to your family's unique needs and circumstances. With this flexibility, you have the power to control the instructions you'll find in this guide to align seamlessly with your personal parenting expedition..

CHAPTER 2:
MONTESSORI FOR BABIES (BIRTH TO 12 MONTHS)

Parenting, from the very beginning, is an extraordinary undertaking, filled with moments of wonder, joy, and love. As new parents, we are entrusted with the profound responsibility of nurturing and guiding our infants through the first delicate months of life. In this chapter, we'll delve into the Montessori approach to parenting babies, a philosophy that not only recognizes the immense potential within each infant but also provides a comprehensive framework for their development. From creating a nurturing Montessori environment for your infant to celebrating the early steps of your journey into this method with your baby, we'll explore how these principles can shape the precious early years of your child's life.

Montessori Magic for Infants: Nurturing Infants With Montessori Love

Our collaboration with Montessori begins in the cradle, where even the tiniest learners are embraced by its principles. At the heart of the philosophy is the belief that infants are born with an innate curiosity and a remarkable ability to learn and adapt to their environment. We'll explore how those principles can be woven into your baby's daily life from the moment they open their eyes to the world. From carefully selected materials that stimulate their senses to designing spaces that promote exploration, we'll walk through the process of setting up your home to match the method. You'll discover how a thoughtfully prepared environment can enhance your baby's natural tendencies to discover and grow.

Early Steps: Parents' Journey Into Montessori With Babies

The amount of discovery and adaptation that parents go through during the first months of their baby is impressive. For this reason, comforting stories from parents who have embarked on their own voyage from the very earliest days with their newborns will be shared. These narratives offer a glimpse into the joys and challenges of integrating the Montessori principles into the daily routine of caring for an infant. Their experiences serve as both inspiration and guidance for those taking their initial steps into the world of Montessori with their babies.

These parents, like you, were initially drawn to this method because of its focus on respecting their child's individuality and fostering a love for learning. Their journeys are a testament to the adaptability and effectiveness of the method's principles for even the youngest members of your family. Their stories will inspire you and provide practical guidance as you embark on your own Montessori adventure with your baby.

Nurturing the Curious Minds of Infants

Montessori principles are not limited by age; they recognize that even the tiniest of humans possess a profound desire to explore and learn. As parents, you have the unique privilege of cultivating this curiosity from day one. Infants have a natural inclination to actively engage with their surroundings. They observe, touch, listen, and begin to make sense of the world around them in their own unique way. Providing opportunities for this exploration is our role as parents, and it comes with a great deal of attentive observation. The more we observe our child with curiosity and care, the more we will know exactly what to put in front of them to further an exciting and passionate discovery of the world.

Now let's delve into the principles and practices of Montessori parenting for infants. We'll explore how to identify and nurture sensitive periods in babies, celebrate the milestones that mark their development, and empower your little ones to take their early steps toward independence.

Embracing the Sensitive Periods in Infancy

Infancy is a time of incredible sensitivity and rapid growth, during which babies are instinctively drawn to specific aspects of their environment. These periods of amplified sensitivity are what we referred to earlier as sensitive periods. In this section, we'll explore how to identify and cultivate these sensitive periods in your baby's life. Real-life stories from parents will provide valuable perspectives and practical tips for supporting your baby during these stages.

Understanding Sensitive Periods

As discussed in Chapter 1, Maria Montessori observed that, during infancy, children experience a series of sensitive periods, each marked by an intense interest and readiness to acquire specific skills or knowledge. These periods are windows of opportunity during which a child's brain is wired to absorb and master particular aspects of their environment.

One aspect of sensitive periods that is important to underline is that they are unique to each child. While there are general tendencies as to when these periods occur, the exact timing can differ. Some infants may show a strong interest in holding objects, while others may be more focused on visual exploration. Recognizing and responding to your baby's individual sensitive periods is key.

Identifying Your Baby's Sensitive Periods

The first step in embracing sensitive periods is to identify them in your baby's behaviors and interests. Pay close attention to what captives your baby's attention and what activities they engage in with enthusiasm. Here are a few common sensitive periods and how you can spot them:

- **Sensory exploration:** During this period, your baby may show a keen interest in exploring their surroundings through touch, taste, and sound. You'll notice them reaching out to grasp objects, putting everything in their mouth, and reacting to different textures and sounds.

- **Language acquisition:** Infants in this sensitive period are particularly receptive to language. They may focus on listening to spoken words, making cooing sounds, and showing an interest in books or other language-rich materials.

- **Visual development:** Babies may go through a sensitive period for visual exploration, where they are fascinated by contrasting colors, patterns, and shapes. They may spend time gazing at mobiles, pictures, or other visually stimulating objects.

- **Fine and gross motor skills:** Some babies show a strong inclination to develop their motor skills during infancy. They may work on reaching for objects, rolling over, or attempting to sit up or crawl.

- **Social interaction:** While babies are not typically known for their social skills, some may enter a sensitive period for social interaction during infancy. They might become more aware of faces, smiles, and social cues.

Cultivating Your Baby's Sensitive Periods

Once you've identified your baby's sensitive periods, the next step is to foster and support their development during these critical phases. Montessori emphasizes the importance of providing the right environment and materials to facilitate learning and exploration.

For example, if your baby is in a sensitive period for sensory exploration, you can offer a variety of safe, age-appropriate tactile experiences, such as different textured fabrics or objects with varying shapes and sizes. This allows them to satisfy their curiosity and refine their sensory perceptions.

If your baby is showing an interest in language acquisition, reading books together, singing songs, and engaging in conversation can be incredibly beneficial. Surround them with language-rich environments and respond to their babbling and cooing with warmth and enthusiasm.

Visual stimulation can be enhanced by introducing simple, contrasting images or mobiles in their line of sight. These can captivate their attention and support their visual development.

Real-Life Stories of Early Development

To further illustrate the impact of embracing sensitive periods in infancy, let's read from parents who have experienced these important stages with their babies.

First, let's hear about Sarah's discovery about her young daughter:

When my daughter Lily reached around six months old, I couldn't help but notice her growing curiosity about the world around her. She seemed particularly interested in grabbing and touching everything she could get her tiny hands on. So, I decided to introduce a variety of textures and objects into her playtime. Soft fabrics, wooden blocks, and even a small tray filled with uncooked rice became her companions on this exploration journey. The joy that spread across Lily's face as she delved into these tactile adventures was something I'll cherish forever. Those moments made me realize the incredible impact of hands-on experiences for young children. Through these simple activities, not only did I witness Lily's fascination with the world, but we also forged a stronger connection as I felt I was making those discoveries along with her.

Mark shares his son's musical experience:

Around Ethan's first birthday, it became abundantly clear that our son had developed an intense fascination with music. He'd drum on whatever he could find, and his eyes would light up at the mere sound of a melody. It was a natural propensity that seemed to be bursting out of him. That's when I decided to orient him to some basic musical instruments, like a xylophone, a little keyboard, and a couple of home-made shakers. The absolute delight on Ethan's face as he created his own sounds was a sight to behold. It dawned on me that by nurturing his love for music during this critical stage of his development, we were not only encouraging his creativity but also helping him conduct his infinite energy in a constructive way. It's a gratifying experience to see the impact of providing just a couple of elements, and see the magic happen by itself.

From Babbling to Baby Steps: Early Achievements

Montessori Milestones in Infancy

Every parent eagerly awaits those magical moments in their baby's life—the first step, the first smile, the first word. Montessori philosophy recognizes these milestones not only as moments of celebration but also as essential steps in a child's development. These achievements represent a baby's growing independence, their ability to interact with the world, and their expanding cognitive and motor skills. In this section, we'll delve into the significance of these achievements and how to encourage motor and sensory development in a Montessori-infused way. We'll explore the joys and challenges of witnessing your baby's early triumphs and the role Montessori plays in nurturing these vital skills. Parent narratives will provide personal accounts of the excitement and wonder that come with these infant milestones.

First, let's put milestones in perspective. We know that in the same way that a particular achievement can spark tremendous joy for parents, it can also cause a great deal of worry and anxiety when it is not happening at a particular time. Because we all form ideas on how and when things should unfold, and because some paediatricians may have a very structured and rigid idea of what a child should be able to do at a particular age, it is only natural for parents to feel anxious at certain stages of their child's development. When this happens, here is a very important reminder:

Your child is unique, and so is their path! There will be times when they are considered "advanced for their age" in a particular area, and "late" or "slow" in other areas of their growth. There will be times when they will appear to have stopped developing completely in an area in which they were once considered to excel. They may even appear to have regressed at some point. This is absolutely normal and true for most if not every child on the planet. Montessori recognizes this phenomenon and respects the pace at which every child advances. Of course, you can reach out for professional opinions when questions arise, and there ARE cases where children would benefit from the special care of a professional at a certain point. But remember that by creating a rich and stimulating environment that allows children to freely explore and learn, and by being a present and caring parent, you are already doing the best you can do for their healthiest and most efficient development as human beings. So, relax, and enjoy the ride, knowing that your child's unique path is not a straight line, and that your natural and innate instinct as a parent will always be there to guide your decisions.

Encouraging Motor and Sensory Development

Moving on to the practical side of things, Montessori-infused parenting places a strong emphasis on fostering motor and sensory development in infants. Here are some key principles to keep in mind as you guide your baby through their early achievements:

- **Providing freedom of movement:** Allow your baby the freedom to move and explore their surroundings. Create a safe space where they can practice rolling over, crawling, and eventually taking those first steps. Montessori principles discourage the use of restraining devices like walkers and encourage a more natural progression of mobility.

- **Simple and purposeful toys:** Choose toys and materials that are simple, aesthetically pleasing, and designed to encourage sensory exploration and fine motor skills. Montessori-inspired toys often include objects for grabbing, textures to touch, and objects that make gentle sounds.

- **Observing and following your baby's lead:** Pay close attention to your baby's signals and interests. If they show a fascination with a particular object or activity, encourage and support their exploration of it. Montessori parenting involves observing your child's preferences and providing opportunities for them to engage in activities that capture their curiosity.

- **Safety and independence:** Create an environment that is safe for your baby to move around in and explore independently. Childproofing your home is essential to ensure your baby's safety while allowing them the freedom to learn through movement and sensory experiences.

First Triumphs: Parent Narratives of Montessori-Infused Infant Milestones

To offer a glimpse into the world of Montessori-infused parenting during these early achievements, below you'll find stories from parents who have embraced this method and its principles in their infants' journeys. These narratives showcase the wonder and pride that come with witnessing your baby's growth and progress.

Emma, mother of a six-month-old, shares her delight in watching her daughter's first attempts at crawling:

We've created a space in our living room with soft mats and a mirror that she loves. It's her special place for practicing her movements. I can see her determination and joy as she gradually learns to crawl. I am often tempted to grab her limbs and do the movements for her, but when I do, I notice that she's not enjoying the process as much, and usually stops trying not long afterwards. Montessori has taught me to trust in her abilities and provide her with the freedom to explore.

Mark and Sarah, parents of twins, share their experience with sensory exploration:

Our twins are fascinated by textures. When we noticed that, Mark pulled out an old yoga mat on which he glued about twenty different pieces of fabrics, carpets, towels, fine grit sandpaper, artificial turf, textured rubber, etc. Saying this was a success would be an understatement. Mark also made it in a way that the mat could be rolled up and carried so that the girls could play anywhere. It has been almost three months now, and the girls are still crawling on it for at least twenty minutes every time we take it out. We are proud to say that many of our parent friends have been inspired by this idea as well.

These parent narratives illustrate the joy and fulfillment that come with nurturing your baby's early achievements through the use of Montessori principles and the use of your own creativity to adapt them to the situation. By following your baby's lead, creating a safe and stimulating environment, and celebrating their milestones, you can embrace the magic of these simple guidelines for parenting during your child's infancy.

Promoting Creativity in the Littlest Minds

Creativity knows no age limit, and the Montessori philosophy recognizes the importance of nurturing creativity in even the tiniest of minds. So, next, we'll delve into activities designed to spark creativity in infants. Although we provide an extensive list of activities at the end of this book, let's have a brief look at a handful of simple examples so as to give us an idea of the spirit behind them. We'll explore the benefits of these creative activities and provide simple variations that parents can implement at home. Personal stories from parents will highlight the joys and discoveries of nurturing creativity in the youngest members of the family.

Benefits of Montessori-Inspired Creativity

Stimulating creativity in babyhood has numerous benefits. It encourages brain development by promoting neuronal connections and cognitive growth. Creative activities also enhance sensory perception, fine and gross motor skills, and emotional development. When infants engage in open-ended creative exploration, they develop problem-solving skills, learn to make choices, and build self-confidence.

Simple At-Home Creativity

Creativity doesn't require elaborate setups or expensive materials. Here are some simple and very cost effective activities to explore your baby's creativity at home:

- **DIY sensory materials:** Create your own sensory materials using everyday items like rice, pasta, or fabric scraps. Fill containers with these materials and let your baby explore their textures.

- **Homemade art supplies:** Make your own baby-friendly paint using natural ingredients like yogurt and food coloring. Ensure your child's safety by using nontoxic materials.

- **Sing and dance:** Sing songs and dance with your baby. This is an excellent bonding activity that encourages movement and rhythm.

- **Nature indoors:** Bring elements of nature indoors. Arrange a small indoor plant or create a mini-garden using safe, child-friendly plants.

- **Sensory Bags:** Create sensory bags using clear, sealable plastic bags filled with safe materials such as colored gel, water, or soft beads. Add sparkling materials in them for a touch of magic! These bags provide visual and tactile stimulation.

- **Light and Shadows:** Position your baby in an area with a focus light, allowing them to experience well-defined shadows. They can be captivated by the interplay of light and shadow on the walls or floor.

The word to remember here is *simplicity*. We don't need to craft elaborate activities or reinvent the wheel every day for babies to be stimulated. Remember that everything is new for them, and a simple empty box of facial tissues can easily become the most fascinating object in the house.

Creative Exploration: Parent Stories

Gemma, a mother of a nine-month-old, shares her experience with sensory play:

I filled a shallow container with uncooked rice and hid small toys inside. It was amazing to see how engaged and focused my baby became while exploring the rice and discovering hidden treasures. I change the objects in the rice every two days or so, and he invariably goes back to check out the container many times a day, eager to discover what new object might be lying there. I'm having a lot of fun with this, and so is my baby boy!

Joe, father of a seven-month-old, talks about their music and movement routine:

Every evening, we play soft music, and my wife and I hold our baby's hands as she "dances." Although she doesn't do anything extraordinary, we're always fascinated by her and excited to see what she'll do next. And every now and then, she surprises us with a new "move" which makes us burst out laughing and cheering. It's not much, but it creates a space for her to try new things. It's become a cherished family ritual that not only brings us closer but also encourages our baby's love for music and movement, and encourages her first creative expressions.

These parenting stories illustrate the joy and simplicity of Montessori-aligned creativity in infancy. By introducing sensory play, art exploration, music, and nature walks into your baby's daily life, you can boost their creative spirit and set the stage for a lifelong love of exploration and self-expression, all while creating precious and cherishable memories.

Montessori at Home: A Creative Environment

Creating a Montessori Haven

The house is where the child will spend most of its time. It's time to get fired up at the idea of using your creativity to create the best possible home environement for your precious little one! In this section, we'll explore the application of the Montessori philosophy to your home, creating a nurturing and creative space that supports your infant's exploration and development. You'll discover practical ways to adapt your home to align with Montessori principles, from designing sensory-rich spaces to selecting age-appropriate materials. Parent stories will showcase the remarkable transformations that can occur when your home becomes a haven for Montessori-inspired exploration and creativity.

Designing Sensory-Rich Spaces

Montessori principles emphasize sensory-rich environments, recognizing that infants learn through their senses. Start by creating designated spaces within your home that cater to your baby's senses. A soft, cozy corner with textured fabrics and age-appropriate books invites tactile exploration. A low mirror hung on the wall allows your baby to discover their reflection, stimulating visual development and self-awareness. A safe sensory board with various textures and interactive elements allows your child to explore and play without any intervention needed on your part, and no cleanup needed afterwards! Again, ensure that these spaces are safe and free from hazards.

Age-Appropriate Materials

Carefully select age-appropriate materials and toys that align with the Montessori philosophy. Opt for toys made from natural materials like wood or cloth. Toys that encourage exploration and problem-solving, such as simple puzzles or stackable blocks, are excellent choices. Rotate toys regularly to maintain your baby's interest and prevent overwhelm. Keep the number of toys limited, focusing on quality over quantity. A low-hanging shelf with a couple of selected toys is strongly encouraged over a fully loaded basket or chest, as it makes each toy seem more interesting and will prevent your child from swimming across a chaotic pool of toys scattered across the room.

Even if your baby has not started crawling yet, an inviting reading corner will not only encourage the parent to pick up books themselves to read with their baby, but it will start fostering curiosity and interest in the child early on, so that when they finally start to move, the book shelf will likely be a place they return to often. Make sure that the books you choose are made as tough as possible. Books that contain very little to no texts are advised, as they encourage parents to be more creative and interactive with their baby, and whereas long texts will usually make your baby lose interest faster. Textured books are highly recommended, as babies and toddlers love them, and they are great for tactile exploration and curiosity.

Floor Beds and Independence

Consider using a floor bed in your baby's room instead of a traditional crib. A floor bed allows your baby to crawl off and on the bed independently, fostering a sense of freedom and autonomy. If your baby moves a lot during sleep and often rolls off the bed by accident, which can be a source of frustration for the baby as well as for the parents, simply surround your baby with more cushions, pillows or tucked blankets. That way your baby will feel comfortably contained and will still be free to crawl off the bed when he feels like it. Ensure the room is babyproofed, so your little explorer can move safely.

Neutral and Natural Decor

Montessori-inspired homes often feature neutral and natural decor. Choose calming colors for your baby's room and play areas. Natural materials like wood, bamboo, jute, wicker, cotton, and wool are preferred over synthetic or plastic materials. Incorporate elements of nature, such as indoor plants, to connect your baby with the natural world. You can even bring elements of the sky and space in the room, with DIY clouds, sun, rainbows, or stars if you wish. Glow-in-the-dark stars on the ceiling are a great way to softly carry your baby to sleep as they usually are very dimmed, slowly fade within an hour or so and are a great source of wonder and fascination for youngsters. Space projectors can also create absolute magical moments before going to sleep with your child. Just make sure not to leave them on during your baby's sleep hours, as their light, noise and electromagnetic fields are elements that can negatively affect the quality of their sleep. Also, it is recommended not to overload your baby's room with a mountain of plushies. The less there are, the more they will cherish and appreciate each one of them. A clutter-free and organized environment facilitates a sense of order and clarity.

Transformative Tales: Parent Stories

Camila, a mother of a seven-months-old and a two-year-old, shares her experience of creating her children's play area:

The main play area for the girls was our tiny living room, which was beginning to feel cramped. So, we decided to transform our studio into a Montessori-inspired play area with soft rugs, low shelves filled with wooden toys, and a beautiful mobile hanging from the ceiling. The change was incredible! Having a well-defined space just for them, our babies became more engaged, independent, and cooperative in their play. My two-year-old is always ready to help her young sister as she understands better how the toys are meant to be played with.

It's a delight watching them play together! I'm amazed to see how a well-prepared environment can make such a difference. Also, the living room is now a much better place to relax together, or focus on activities that don't require any material, like dancing, singing, exercising, etc.

David, father of a nine-month-old, discusses their use of a floor bed:

We transitioned to a floor bed when our baby started crawling, and it worked like a charm! When his nap is over, he often silently crawls out of his bed and starts playing around on his own, which is fantastic to watch in my opinion. I know some parents aren't comfortable with that, but if you're confident that you did a good job babyproofing their room, it's a great opportunity for them to start building autonomy and confidence very early on. Also, I love that I can lay beside my baby and read stories before sleep, without having to move him around too much after he falls asleep. For me personally, the experience has been a hundred percent positive, and I totally recommend it.

Karina, a mother of a 18 months-old, has chosen to include a jade plant (Crassula ovata) in her baby's room:

Incorporating a jade plant into my baby boy's room turned out to be a brilliant idea. The original intention was to have a plant with detoxifying properties in the room to improve the quality of the air, but it turned out to be a lot more than that. I took the time with my baby boy to show him how to touch the plant with care, emphasizing on its fragility. Then we watered it together, and even petted it, just as I showed him how to do with the dog ha ha! I think he understands that the plant is a living thing as well, and it needs love and care like we do. Now he points the plant to me almost every single day, so that we can take care of it together. I'm very proud to see the first seeds of empathy and loving care sprouting in my little baby!

These transformative tales from parents underscore the positive impact on your infant of creating a Montessori-inspired environment at home. By designing sensory-rich spaces, selecting age-appropriate materials, embracing floor beds, choosing neutral colors, and incorporating elements of nature, you can provide your baby with an atmosphere that nurtures their curiosity, independence, and caring for other living things.

As you embark on this Montessori adventure at home, remember that it's not about perfection but progress. Adapt the Montessori principles to suit your family's unique needs and circumstances, and enjoy the process of watching your baby blossom in an environment that celebrates their innate potential. Your home can become a place of wonder, exploration, and evolution, where the foundations of a lifelong passion for education and autonomy are lovingly laid.

CHAPTER 3:
MONTESSORI FOR TODDLERS (12-36 MONTHS)

Among the school material small children enjoy most are the frames with two pieces of cloth — some have buttons and buttonholes, others ribbons, hooks and eyes, and shoe buttons — and it is delightful to watch the toddlers doing up buttons and tying bows with tremendous concentration. —Maria Montessori

The Toddler Years: Challenges and Opportunities

As we enter the world of toddlers, we find ourselves faced with a whirlwind of curiosity, energy, and endless questions. This chapter introduces you to the Montessori approach to toddlerhood, offering insights into how Maria Montessori's philosophy aligns with the unique characteristics of this age group.

We'll explore the toddler mind from this philosophical perspective and learn how to navigate the challenges of this stage with wisdom and grace. Real-life anecdotes from other Montessori parents will illustrate the beauty and triumphs of embracing these principles during the toddler years.

Maria Montessori underscored the importance of fostering independence, self-discovery, and love of learning from the earliest years of a child's life. Toddlers in particular are poised at the precipice of independence, desiring to declare their newfound abilities and explore their burgeoning sense of self. Within these pages, we will explore together how Montessori practices can facilitate this process, nurturing the natural inclinations of toddlers while cultivating an environment that encourages their innate curiosity and thirst for knowledge.

Andrina, mother of a three-year-old boy, shares her experience with her toddler:

Things are going really well with our son, to be honest. The little one's been showing real independence, sorting themselves out, and even taking on puzzles like a champ. Montessori's discipline tricks have been handy for dealing with the occasional tantrum. We hardly felt the famous "terrible two" that many people talk about. All in all, it's been a rich and pleasant experience, and my husband and I are grateful to have a child that responds well to the Montessori guidelines.

In the sections that follow, we will delve deeper into the practical applications of Montessori principles for toddlers, offering guidance on setting up a prepared climate at home, selecting age-appropriate materials, and fostering respectful and nurturing interactions. The goal is to empower you with the knowledge and tools needed to embark on this exciting expedition through toddlerhood with wisdom and grace, ultimately promoting a strong foundation for your child's future maturation and development.

Montessori-Infused Discipline for Happy Toddlers

Toddlers, characterized by their insatiable curiosity and innate drive for exploration, are truly a source of wonder. They find themselves in a stage of life where every moment presents an opportunity for discoveries, and their energy knows no limits. Nevertheless, it's no secret that toddlers are notorious for their inclination to test boundaries and push limits. We'll therefore start by embarking on a comprehensive exploration of the Montessori discipline principles, providing a practical guide for effectively managing toddler behavior while nurturing their emerging independence and self-regulation skills.

The Montessori approach to discipline, rooted in respect and comprehension, acknowledges that children possess an intrinsic motivation for learning and growth. It views discipline as a guiding force that assists children in navigating the complexities of their world. The Montessori philosophy encourages parents to assume the role of gentle guides, encouraging a sense of responsibility and self-discipline in toddlers. Parents can promote the development of vital life skills like self-control and problem-solving by empathetically and patiently addressing challenging behaviors in their toddlers, and by understanding their unique developmental needs.

Toddlers are in full exploration mode, which means that they will learn boundaries and limits by going beyond them. Your role as parents is to be as clear and consistent as possible, so that the toddler who goes beyond a certain limit already knows and expects a response from his parents. It's also important to note that wanting to discover what the consequences are for crossing boundaries is also a part of the exploration! This is nothing to be taken personal for parents, it is completely natural and part of the process of boundaries exploration. Moreover, toddlers are still complete beginners at managing their emotions, which means that meltdowns and tantrums for apparently silly reasons are par for the course and will inevitably happen. Let's look at what the application of Montessori guidelines would like when a tantrum does happen.

Dealing with Tantrums

In order to offer an empathetic and appropriate response to a toddler going through an intense emotional discharge, it's important to remember a few things about what they are going through.

First off, the full-on display of their emotions means that we have created an environment where they feel safe enough for them to express their feelings in this way, and that alone is a win for the parent.

Secondly, toddlers have not learned to regulate the powerful emotions going through their tiny bodies yet. Not only is it something new for them, but the sheer power of those feelings will leave them completely overwhelmed and disoriented at times. Trying to reason with a toddler while emotions are bursting out of them will often prove futile and counterproductive. When children are in the middle of a crisis, all they perceive and understand from us is the kind of energy we direct at them. If they sense that we are angry, it will add fuel to the fire and give them even more emotion to deal with. We may find silence quickly through agression, but this way of dealing with tantrums will foster emotional and psychological challenges that we and the child will have to deal with sooner or later.

The only appropriate response then is to come alongside the child, to make them feel like we are still on the same side, even if the parent is the one who sparked their emotional response in the first place. We can opt for a gentle hand on their back or shoulder, a soft and reassuring voice, or whatever feels natural in the moment. The idea is to give them the sense that we understand what they are going through, that it is okay and normal to feel this way, that we will be there the whole time, and that everything is going to be okay. The easier we make this process of emotional regulation for them, the faster they will get good at it, and the less frequent and intense those situations are likely to be in the future.

During their distress, we may feel inclined to change our mind and give in to their demand so that they stop crying right away, but that would not be of service to us nor the child in the long run. What children want more than anything is to know that their parents are strong and loving no matter what. They want to have parents that they respect, much more than parents who will give in easily to their demands. Plus, when a child feels safe, supported, and stimulated within clear boundaries set by the parents, tantrums will be more rare and relatively easy to deal with.

Once again, Montessori teaches us to set up the right environment in which the magic that is already present within the child can take place. It's not about doing more for the child, it's about doing the right thing, sitting back, and letting things happen, with minimal intervention, which, in the end, actually means doing less. This is the power and simplicity of the Montessori Method.

Matthew, parent of a toddler, shares his opinion about discipline and tantrums:

> *Tantrums used to leave us all feeling drained and disconnected. Montessori has taught us to be more patient and understanding. When our child throws a tantrum, we now see it as an opportunity for growth—a chance to connect and guide them through their emotions. I'm not saying everything is cream and peaches now, but we no longer experience these situations in a heavy and negative way anymore, and we feel we are growing too as parents.*

Throughout this chapter, we will explore stories shared by parents who have successfully implemented Montessori discipline methods in their own homes. These real-life stories will provide insights and practical examples of how regulations can be applied to create a harmonious home environment. From handling tantrums to encouraging cooperation, these anecdotes will offer a glimpse into the transformative power of Montessori discipline.

As you embark on your journey through the toddler years with the Montessori method, you will gain a deeper fondness for its profound influence on your child's behavior and growth. By embracing a philosophy grounded in respect, empathy, and the motivation of independence, you will not only navigate the challenges of toddlerhood more effectively, but will also lay a solid foundation for your child's future growth and learning. This section will equip you with the knowledge and discernment required to embrace the joys and complexities of toddlerhood within the framework of Montessori principles.

Building Language and Communication Skills

Language development is a fascinating journey for toddlers, and the Montessori approach recognizes its crucial role in their overall growth. Techniques for promoting language development in this age group focus on creating a rich and stimulating environment where children can explore and expand their vocabulary naturally.

Creating a Language-Rich Environment

Montessori emphasizes the importance of a language-rich environment for kids. Surrounding your toddler with books, conversation, and language-based experiences can deeply enhance their linguistic skills. Reading to your child daily, even for just a few minutes, exposes them to new words and concepts. Select age-appropriate books with vibrant images and engaging stories to captivate their interest.

Parents are encouraged to provide opportunities for self-expression through language. Motivate your toddler to express their thoughts and feelings, even if they are just starting to form words. Listen actively and respond with enthusiasm; this will reinforce their attempts at communication. However, avoid correcting their pronunciation or grammar; instead, provide a model for clear and correct speech by repeating their words and phrases slowly and correctly.

Developing Vocabulary Through Practical Life Activities

Practical life activities play a significant role in speech development. Engaging your toddler in daily activities, such as cooking or dressing, offers a natural context for learning new words. Use precise and simple language to describe each step of the activity, introducing relevant vocabulary. For example, during meal preparation you can introduce words like "spoon," "mix," and "stir."

Enhancing Communication Techniques

Effective communication is a two-way street, and it is important to practice clear and empathetic communication with your child. Maintain eye contact when speaking to them, use simple and concise sentences, and pause to give them time to respond. Encourage them to repeat or comment on what they've heard, which not only reinforces their understanding but also helps build their expressive language skills.

Sometimes, however, when a child is under an intense deal of emotion, words can become utterly useless. Chloe, a mother who embraced the Montessori philosophy a few years ago, gives us a great example of "less is more", when it comes to communication and discipline:

I remember that day, he threw a tantrum because he wanted chocolate before going to bed, something I didn't allow. He was on the floor, crying like crazy. My old reflex would have been to justify myself, convince him that his reaction made no sense, and make him stop right away. But this time, I calmly sat beside him, and softly rubbed his back and shoulders while taking very deep breaths. I breathed a little louder than I would have if I was on my own, as to invite him to calm down with me whenever he would feel ready. I wanted him to sense that even though I didn't give in to his desire, I still had his back, and we were on the same team. After a few minutes, he started to settle, and finished the remainder of his crying in my arms. Once the crying had stopped completely and his breathing returned to normal, I asked him in a loving and kind voice if he wanted me to read stories in bed before going to sleep. He said yes. And that was the end of it. I was prepared to discuss what had just happened with him, but it didn't seem necessary. Even though this went exactly as I intended, I was still shocked at how powerful this simple technique proved to be... and I practically said nothing! It doesn't always go that smoothly of course, but I think that most of the time, we rationalize and speak too much, and it only makes the situation worse. I see now that even though children may feel angry for not getting what they want, deep down they prefer hav-

ing an unwavering and confident captain of the ship as a parent over a mommy that always says yes.

Parental Involvement and Stories of Success

Next, you'll find stories shared by parents who have adopted Montessori techniques for language development. These anecdotes serve as a source of inspiration, illustrating the positive impact of fostering successful language development in toddlers. From the first attempts at coherent speech to engaging in meaningful conversations, you'll witness the remarkable progress that can be achieved through the Montessori approach.

Samantha, a Montessori parent, comments on her experience of using the method to develop her child's communication skills:

Using Montessori methods for our toddler's language development has made a big difference. Montessori taught me to really listen, praise my child's efforts, and create a proper space for verbal articulation. We began reading together every day and night before bed, which ignited interest and self-expression, with my son asking me questions about the book characters and even speculating about what would happen next. Everyday tasks like baking also helped me introduce new words into his routine. It's wonderful to see your child learning this fast without any pressure; all we got to do is provide a little spark!

Keith shares his experience of arguments after embracing the Montessori method. Although Keith's son is no longer a toddler as Keith tells this story, it serves as a great example of the kind of communication skills we want to encourage in our children of all ages:

Teaching our son respectful listening through Montessori principles has been a revelation in our household. Instead of occasional arguments escalating into nightmares, we now experience respectful conversations. For many months, we used every occasion we had to put forth the reminder that everybody's point of view is valid and ought to be heard and respected. To illustrate the point that there can be many possible perspectives on a subject, and that although they may differ, they can equally be valid, I like to use a simple wooden cube that has different coloured faces on it. I put it between me and my kid and ask him to tell me what colour the cube is. Then I tell him what I see. Then I take the cube and tell him something like: "See? We may see different things, yet we are looking at the same object. And every situation is exactly like this cube: there are many different ways to look at them. So next time somebody has a different opinion than you about something, remember that he may simply be seeing another face of the cube. That doesn't mean his point of view is wrong, it may just be different, and we can learn from it! So, the best thing to do is always to listen and try to understand, rather than judge." I don't know if that particular image would work for any child, but it has certainly hit home with ours. Our son has now learned to truly listen to our perspectives and express his thoughts calmly, knowing that his perspective will be listened to as well. This transformation has not only eased conflicts but has also strengthened our family's bonds, as we all feel heard and valued. I think it works because it goes both ways. If we think our children's point of view is less valuable than ours because we are adults, they will immediately feel it and things will go sideways pretty fast. So, we have to embrace it ourselves before we can teach it to our children. Montessori's emphasis on communication skills has had a profound impact on our daily interactions, turning potential disagreements into opportunities for growth and understanding, and we are super thankful for it.

By exploring Montessori strategies for language development, and effective communication, you'll be well-equipped to promote your toddler's linguistic and social skills, and support their journey toward becoming confident communicators. Remember that every child progresses at their own pace, and the key is to provide a rich and encouraging environment that allows them to thrive and learn at their pace.

Nurturing Independence and Creativity

Practical Life Skills for Independent Toddlers

Independence: the core of Montessori philosophy. It's a principle that begins to take root in the toddler years, recognizing that even the youngest children have an innate desire to do things for themselves, and that, by nurturing this desire, parents can lay a strong foundation for their children's future independence.

One way to foster independence in toddlers is through practical life activities. These activities are designed to mimic everyday tasks that adults do, allowing children to learn essential life skills while also developing a sense of responsibility and capability. For example, toddlers can learn to pour their own water, dress themselves, or even help with simple meal preparations like spreading peanut butter on bread—simple things that have big repercussions.

These activities may seem small, but they have a profound impact on a toddler's sense of self. When a child can pour their own drink or button their own shirt, they experience a wave of confidence and independence. They begin to see themselves as capable individuals who can take care of their own needs.

One of the key principles of Montessori practical life exercises is that they are designed to be child-sized. This means that the materials and tools used are specifically chosen to fit the child's hands and abilities. For example, a child-sized pitcher and glass are much easier for a toddler to manipulate than adult-sized ones. This child-centered approach allows toddlers to engage in these activities successfully and unassisted.

As parents, witnessing our toddlers taking their first steps toward independence is a remarkable experience. It's a testament to the power of Montessori principles in action. Parents often share stories of their toddlers proudly pouring their own cereal or putting on their shoes, and these moments are not just about the task itself but about the confidence and sense of accomplishment it instills in the child.

Meet Janice, a dedicated Montessori parent who has embraced the philosophy in her home. One day, she had a heartwarming experience that beautifully illustrated the power of Montessori principles in fostering independence and creativity in her toddler:

> As a mother, I cannot describe the feeling of witnessing your child doing something by themselves. The day I saw my son putting on his shoes without any help, I felt so proud and joyful that a tear rolled down my cheek. I called my husband so he could appreciate the scene and immediately felt we were going in the right direction. It was hard for us to decide which way to go when our son was born, as there were so many options and opinions that made us so confused. My husband and I were both raised in a strict and pushy environment where once our father decided it was time, we did something by ourselves, he wouldn't let go until we achieved it. It worked but involved a lot of stress and crying and shouting. What worried us a bit about Montessori is that we thought if we didn't push our child to do a particular thing, he would never do it. However, seeing that my son is three years old and he just tied his shoes successfully without asking for any help, I'm positive we chose the right path.

Montessori-Inspired Play-Based Learning

Toddlers are naturally curious, and Montessori education capitalizes on this innate quality. Let's explore how Montessori-inspired play-based learning can satiate the curiosity and thirst for learning of these young minds.

Toddlers can learn through play in numerous ways, as play is an essential part of their cognitive, physical, and social development. Although you will find an extensive list of activities for toddlers at the end of the book, let's look at some more general examples of how toddlers can learn through play:

- **Pretend Play**: Toddlers often engage in pretend play, such as playing house or using dolls and action figures. Through these activities, they learn about roles, relationships, and social interactions. They also develop their imagination and creativity.

- **Building with Blocks**: Building with blocks helps toddlers develop fine motor skills, spatial awareness, and problem-solving abilities. They learn about balance, symmetry, gravity, general physics principles, and cause-and-effect relationships by constructing and knocking down structures.

- **Art and Creativity**: Activities like drawing, coloring, and finger painting encourage creativity and self-expression. Toddlers can explore colors, shapes, and textures while also developing their fine motor skills.

- **Outdoor Play**: Outdoor play in a playground or natural environment helps toddlers develop physical skills like running, jumping, climbing, and balancing. It also exposes them to nature, teaching them about the environment and different sensory experiences.

- **Sensory Play**: Activities involving sensory materials like sand, water, playdough, and sensory bins help toddlers explore their five senses. They learn about texture, temperature, weight, and how different materials can be manipulated.

- **Puzzles and Sorting**: Simple puzzles and sorting games help toddlers with problem-solving and cognitive development. They learn to recognize shapes, patterns, and matching skills.

- **Listening to Stories**: Reading books or telling stories to toddlers introduces them to language, vocabulary, and narrative structure. It promotes early literacy and a love for reading.

- **Musical Play**: Singing songs, playing musical instruments, or dancing to music helps toddlers develop rhythm, coordination, and an appreciation for music. It also encourages self-expression.

- **Role-Playing**: Encouraging toddlers to take on different roles, such as pretending to be a doctor, chef, or firefighter, fosters imagination and social skills. They learn about different professions and social roles.

- **Nature Exploration**: Going on nature walks or exploring the outdoors allows toddlers to learn about the natural world, different plants, insects, and animals. They can also discover scientific concepts like cause and effect and observation.

- **Puppet Play**: Using puppets or stuffed animals, toddlers can create scenarios and engage in storytelling. This activity enhances communication skills, creativity, and emotional expression.

- **Cooking or Baking**: Involving toddlers in simple cooking or baking activities teaches them about measurements, counting, and following instructions. It also introduces them to basic culinary skills.

- **Water Play**: Water play in a tub or with water tables allows toddlers to experiment with pouring, floating, sinking, and measuring. It's an excellent way to teach basic science concepts.

- **Problem-Solving Board Games**: Simple board games like matching games or memory games help toddlers develop cognitive skills, including memory, pattern recognition, and decision-making.

- **Social Play**: Playing with peers and siblings helps toddlers learn important social skills like sharing, taking turns, and resolving conflicts. They practice communication and empathy.

These examples help us see clearly that play is an integral part of a toddler's development, promoting physical, cognitive, emotional, and social growth. It's through play that they make sense of the world around them and acquire valuable skills that lay the foundation for future learning.

Outdoor Adventures and Nature-Based Activities

As parents, we often marvel at the surprise and curiosity that toddlers show toward the natural world. If we are open to it, it can also be a great opportunity for us to rediscover the wonders of Nature through the eyes of our child, but with the added layer of understanding that our adult mind provides us. We can marvel again at the endless combination of shapes, colours, and textures that surrounds us, understanding that so many evolution processes had to happen for all of this to flourish! We can be in awe at the innate intelligence and beauty that is embedded in every rock, plant, and creature, thus crafting countless sceneries of perfect harmony and balance. Nature is the ultimate artist and engineer, and toddlers will internalize even more of its gifts, if guided by a parent who is willing to be open and curious too. By incorporating Montessori principles and by living them as parents as well, we can encourage their natural sense of exploration and foster a connection with nature that will last a lifetime.

There are many benefits to outdoor play, which can provide a range of exciting activities to ignite your toddler's imagination. From a nature scavenger hunt to a simple exploration of the natural world present in your backyard, each experience can help your child develop a deep appreciation for the world around them. Spending time in Nature also helps humans regulate and rebalance a myriad of metabolic functions, and this is especially beneficial for young children who go through so many physiological and psychological changes at the same time. The more they spend time outside, the more their quality of sleep, digestion, mood, mental focus, and overall health will regulate and improve. Consistent exposure to Nature is surely one of the simplest, and greatest gifts you can offer your child on the beginning of his life.

Creating a Nurturing Montessori Home

With our lungs full of fresh air, and our bodies recalibrated from our precious time spent outside, let's go back inside our beloved shelter and take another look at how we can further optimize our space to make it even more nourishing for our precious littles ones.

Emily, a Montessori parent, shares her experience of embracing the method's principles in her family's home environment:

Turning our home into a Montessori-inspired space has been quite the journey, and, I must say, it's been incredibly rewarding. We've observed our little one's independence and creativity really come to life in this setup. With the thoughtfully chosen learning tools and child-sized furniture, our home has become a hub of exploration and discovery. My life partner is not a handyman at all, but when we started discussing how we were going to turn our home around with the Montessori guidelines in mind, he became really involved. Most of our discussions at night revolved around new ideas and DIY projects for the house. I was really surprised at how motivated he became. He watched tons of DIY videos, figured things out mostly by himself, and finally did a surprisingly good job at realizing our projects. I'm grateful that just a few Montessori principles made life in the house so much more enjoyable for everybody and have just naturally become a part of our everyday life. Making a few sound changes can really make parenting a joyful adventure where all of us, including our child, can grow and learn in a very pleasant way.

Montessori principles emphasize the importance of an environment that supports a child's natural development. Here are key considerations for curating a toddler-friendly Montessori home:

- **Accessible learning materials:** Keep age-appropriate learning materials within easy reach. This encourages your toddler to independently choose and engage with activities that pique their interest.

- **Child-sized furniture:** Toddler-sized tables, chairs, and shelves make it easier for your little one to access their belongings, fostering a sense of ownership and responsibility.

- **Order and simplicity:** Maintain an organized and clutter-free environment. Having designated spaces for toys and activities aids concentration and teaches your toddler the value of tidiness.

- **Natural materials:** As mentioned in previous chapters, opt for toys and materials made from natural substances like wood and fabric. These provide sensory-rich experiences and promote sustainability.

- **Defined spaces:** Create specific areas for different activities, such as a reading nook, art corner, or practical life activity station. Clearly defined spaces help your toddler understand the purpose of each area and encourage independence.

- **Toy rotation:** Instead of overwhelming your child with multiple toys, consider rotating them. This keeps the environment fresh and invites deeper exploration and engagement.

- **Artistic expression:** Set up an art corner with easily accessible supplies like crayons, paper, and child-safe scissors. Encourage your toddler's creative expression through art.

- **Connection with nature:** Incorporate elements of nature into your home, such as houseplants or nature-inspired artwork. Nature has a calming effect on children and stimulates curiosity and creativity.

By applying Montessori principles to your home environment, you'll create a space that inspires your toddler to explore, create, and learn independently. As your child progresses through this stage of development, having a home that aligns with the Montessori philosophy will provide them with the freedom and support they need to thrive.

Parent Testimonial

Let's finish this chapter by exploring Malorie's experience. She's a mother of triplets who implemented an art corner for her kids as a way to inspire their creativity and freedom. She knew that fostering a love for art and self-expression from a young age was essential, and Montessori principles offered the perfect framework for this endeavor.

With three toddlers at home, chaos was sometimes the order of the day. But Malorie was determined to create a dedicated space where her children, Lily, Max, and Ava, could explore their artistic talents freely. She carefully designed the art corner with child-sized tables and chairs and low shelves stocked with art supplies.

The transformation was remarkable. The triplets took to their art corner with uncontrolled enthusiasm. They independently selected their materials, experimented with colors and textures, and crafted their mini-masterpieces. Malorie marveled at how each of her children had a unique approach to art, even at such a tender age.

Montessori encouraged Malorie to step back and allow her triplets to take the lead in their creative works. She noticed how they gained confidence with each brushstroke and were eager to share their artwork with anyone who would listen.

"Implementing the art corner was like watching a mini-revolution in our home," Malorie explains. "Not only did it keep them engaged for hours, but it also taught them patience, focus, and the value of self-expression."

As the triplets continued to explore their art corner, Malorie saw their independence and creativity flower. This took some time, but they eventually learned to clean up after themselves, take care of their art supplies, and even began teaching each other new techniques they'd discovered.

"Our art corner has become not only a place of creativity but also a space where my children learn to express themselves, cooperate, and develop essential life skills. It's a testament to the power of Montessori principles in nurturing confident and independent little artists."

Malorie's experience with her triplets and their Montessori-inspired art corner demonstrates the profound effect a well-designed environment can have on a child's development.

In the upcoming chapter, we'll take a closer look at the concept of responsibility and its significance in getting children ready for their preschool journey. We'll examine how Montessori principles empower young learners to embrace responsibilities with confidence and independence and provide parents with valuable insights into how to encourage self-reliance and autonomy in their children. The focus is on using the Montessori philosophy to lay a strong foundation for the transition to preschool, and how the method can continue to shape and guide children as they move forward on their educational path.

CHAPTER 4:
MONTESSORI FOR PRESCHOOLERS (THREE TO FIVE YEARS)

I have said enough if I have persuaded you to undertake for yourself the interesting experiment of a visit to one of our schools to watch the happy little ones at work. —Maria Montessori

Preparing for School and Life

Montessori preschool principles lay the essential groundwork for lifelong learning and success. At this stage, children not only acquire academic knowledge but also build critical life skills and develop a deep love for learning that will serve them well in the years ahead. Montessori's child-centered approach fosters independence, curiosity, and self-confidence, ensuring that children are well-prepared for the challenges and opportunities they will encounter in school and life.

One of the fundamental aspects of Montessori preschool is the emphasis on self-directed learning. Children are encouraged to explore their personal interests and engage in activities that capture their curiosity. This approach not only makes learning enjoyable but also instills a sense of responsibility for their education—a vital skill for success in school and beyond.

Montessori Preschool: The Foundation for Success

In this chapter, we will discuss the Montessori principles applied to children aged three to five. Although I will often refer to Montessori preschools, the same principles apply when parents are doing Montessori at home for their preschooler.

Montessori preschools create an environment that promotes autonomy. Children learn to make choices, solve problems, and take ownership of their actions. These skills will be invaluable as they progress through their educational journey and eventually enter the world as confident and self-sufficient individuals.

Parents' stories offer inspiring insights into the profound impact of Montessori preschool experiences. They share how their children's curiosity was ignited, how they developed a strong work ethic, and how they flourished academically and socially. These narratives serve as a testament to the effectiveness of the Montessori approach in preparing children for success.

As we explore the principles and practices of Montessori preschool in this chapter, you'll gain a deeper understanding of how this foundation sets the stage for a lifetime of achievement and fulfillment. Whether you're a parent considering Montessori preschool for your child or seeking to better understand its long-term benefits, the stories and insights shared here will illuminate the transformative power of this educational philosophy.

Audrey, a Montessori parent, shares her story:

> *As the mother of a bright and inquisitive child, I was determined to provide the best possible start to my daughter's educational journey. That's when I discovered the wonders of Montessori preschool. Little did I know just how profoundly it would shape her path to success.*

From the moment my daughter stepped into her Montessori preschool, I could see the difference. The classroom was a captivating environment filled with materials that begged to be explored. But it wasn't just about the materials; it was the philosophy and the staff behind them that truly made a world of difference.

In the Montessori classroom, my daughter was encouraged to follow her interests and passions. She could choose her activities, dive deeply into subjects that fascinated her, and set her own pace for learning. This approach not only kindled her love for learning but also taught her a fundamental skill: the ability to take charge of her education.

From an early age, she learned to be responsible for her tasks, to tidy up after herself, and to work collaboratively with her peers. These skills have translated into a strong work ethic, remarkable problem-solving abilities, and an impressive sense of self-assurance.

But perhaps the most significant impact of Montessori preschool was how it prepared my daughter for the formal school years and, ultimately, for life. She entered kindergarten with a sense of excitement and a genuine love for learning that set her apart from her peers. Her confidence, curiosity, and respect for others were evident in everything she did.

Today, as I watch my daughter excel in school and approach challenges with grace and determination, I can't help but credit her Montessori preschool experience. It wasn't just a stepping stone; it was the foundation upon which she grew into a strong woman.

Montessori principles have not only shaped my daughter's educational journey but also her character. I am immensely grateful for the profound impact the school had on her life, and I wholeheartedly recommend it to any parent seeking to prepare their little ones for a future filled with promise and achievement.

Independence, Responsibility and Self-Direction

In Montessori preschools, children are given a degree of autonomy that might surprise some parents. They are allowed to choose their own activities, work at their own pace, and even initiate their own learning experiences. This level of freedom fosters a sense of responsibility and self-direction that becomes invaluable as they progress in their educational path.

Montessori preschoolers quickly learn to manage their time, organize their workspace, and make decisions about what interests them the most. The act of choosing, whether it's selecting a particular puzzle, a book, or a creative project, encourages them to think critically, prioritize, and take ownership of their learning.

Encouraging children to exercise their freedom of choice is closely related to the fact that this freedom is attached to certain responsibilities. For example, it's important to teach children that after they finish playing or using a game, they should leave everything organized or properly set up for the next child to use.

This emphasis on social consideration promotes a mix of freedom plus responsibility, enabling both social awareness and self-direction in children. As they become familiar with these routines, they gradually take ownership of their actions, striking a balance between personal choices and the needs of the larger group. This approach plays a crucial role in nurturing responsible and socially conscious individuals.

Montessori Beyond Preschool: A Lifelong Journey

Transitioning From Montessori Preschool to Mainstream Education

The shift from Montessori preschool to a more traditional educational setting marks a crucial juncture in a child's academic journey. Understandably, a parent may have concerns about how well their children will navigate this transition. However, it's truly remarkable how seamlessly and flawlessly Montessori preschool graduates make this leap. Their experience with the Montessori method grants them a tough set of life skills, including independence and innate self-motivation. These competencies are not just valuable; they are essential assets as they take on new challenges within mainstream educational environments.

What stands out about Montessori children is their insatiable curiosity and self-driven desire to explore and obtain knowledge. This genuine love for learning becomes a trait that exponentially boosts their education, enabling better and complete development in each sensitive period. Furthermore, their autonomy ensures they have the confidence to approach new subjects or tasks with an incredible sense of ownership and resilience.

It's important to mention that the child will invariably have to adapt to certain changes in the way things are done in mainstream establishments. The most noticeable change perhaps is the rigidity of schedules and timelines that Montessori children, who are accustomed to learning at their own pace, will have to get used to. This may seem like a big hurdle at first glance, but the way most kids experience it is in fact very positive. Having already developped a strong confidence and capacity to adapt, changes like these are actually welcomed by the children as an exciting new way to test their skills and a motivating force to get better in certain areas. Once again, the versatility of a Montessori upbringing proves to be an invaluable asset.

Transitioning from one school type to another is not merely a matter of adaptation; it's an opportunity and a challenge that will make your children flourish, armed with the tools developed in their own homes.

Montessori for Life: Stories of Lifelong Montessori Learners

To illustrate the lasting impact of Montessori principles, let's take a look at some famous lifelong Montessori learners (Anthony, 2023):

- Jeff Bezos, CEO of Amazon, is a compelling case study highlighting the profound impact of a Montessori education. His mother, as reported in *The Wall Street Journal*, has expressed how Bezos greatly benefited from the self-directed learning opportunities that a Montessori classroom offers.

- Gabriel García Márquez, a Nobel Prize-winning author, acknowledges that his Montessori education played a crucial role in nurturing his passion for writing. He is famously quoted as expressing this sentiment: "I don't think there's a better method than Montessori for nurturing children's sensitivity to the wonders of the world and igniting their inquisitiveness about the mysteries of life."

- Dakota Fanning, recognized as the youngest-ever nominee for a Screen Actors Guild Award, has mentioned that she acquired reading skills at the age of two during her time in a Montessori school. This educational setting granted her the liberty to explore her early interests, particularly her passion for reading, and cultivated a level of concentration that proved valuable in her acting profession.

- Taylor Swift, a Grammy Award-winning artist celebrated in the domain of country and pop music, received her early education at a Montessori school. She is acknowledged for embodying the attributes of independence, self-awareness, and creativity that are nurtured within the Montessori educational environment.

These stories emphasize the continuing impact of Montessori schooling, which extends far beyond the preschool years. The method's principles instill in children a lifelong love for learning, the ability to adapt to new environments, and the confidence to pursue their passions.

As a parent, you can contribute to fostering these values in your child's life, whether they're embarking on their first day of preschool or venturing on to higher education. Maria Montessori's ideology is a lifelong companion on the journey of self-discovery and personal growth.

Exploring Science and Nature With Young Scientists

Montessori education places a strong emphasis on science and nature activities as catalysts for nurturing a child's natural curiosity. Within this approach, science serves not only as a subject but also as a means to develop a deep interest in understanding the world around us.

The activities below are thoughtfully designed to encourage hands-on exploration and keen observation. Via the use of various materials and tools, children are prompted to directly engage with the natural world, whether it involves examining leaves, exploring the life cycle of a butterfly, or experimenting with the properties of water.

Montessori-Inspired Science and Nature Activities

One captivating experiment is the "magic milk" experiment. Children can set up a shallow dish of whole milk and add a few drops of food coloring. Then, using a cotton swab dipped in dish soap, they can touch the milk's surface. This simple experiment demonstrates the reaction between the soap and the fat molecules in the milk, causing the colors to swirl and mix and creating a fascinating display of science in action.

Furthermore, children can explore the world of botany by planting seeds, nurturing seedlings, and observing plant growth. This hands-on experience teaches them about plant life cycles, responsibility, and the importance of caring for living organisms. Moreover, bird watching remains a cherished activity, where youngsters set up bird feeders to attract and observe different bird species, deepening their understanding of wildlife and ecology.

Another exciting activity involves using baking soda and vinegar. Children can mix a small amount of baking soda with white vinegar in a container. The resulting chemical reaction produces fizzing and bubbling, showcasing the release of carbon dioxide gas. This experiment not only introduces basic chemical reactions but also instills in the child the idea that there are magical phenomenons out there to discover,

Nature journals and outdoor art encourage creative expression while allowing children to document their outdoor experiences and observations.

In summary, science and nature activities offer a holistic approach to learning, boosting curiosity, critical thinking, and a deeper connection to the wild. These activities provide a bunch of opportunities for children to explore, experiment, and discover the beauty and wonder of the world around them.

Encouraging Hands-On Exploration and Discovery

One key aspect of the Montessori approach is the development of essential skills in observation and inference. Children learn to closely observe their surroundings and draw logical conclusions from their observations. These skills not only underpin scientific inquiry but also enhance critical thinking abilities that extend beyond the boundaries of scientific exploration.

As parents, you can empower your children to pursue their own interests and questions, resulting in a personalized and profoundly fascinating learning experience. This technique promotes a genuine hunger for understanding the world as children explore topics that genuinely captivate them.

In addition, these activities seamlessly integrate with other aspects of your child's education, allowing the skills cultivated in science to be applied across various areas of knowledge, including history, language, and math. This interdisciplinary approach enhances your child's overall educational experience by facilitating significant connections between different fields of education.

As parents, it's crucial to recognize that learning extends beyond the classroom, with nature itself serving as a dynamic educational space. Outdoor adventures and nature studies should be integral components of your child's upbringing, enabling them to develop a deep fondness for the environment and a sense of responsibility toward its preservation.

Scientific Adventures

Hanna, mother of a seven-year-old girl, shares an anecdote about her daughter using her basic scientific knowledge to save a butterfly:

> *Observing my daughter's gentle rescue of a fragile butterfly one rainy afternoon was a moment that left a profound impression. As she cradled the delicate creature in her hands, her eyes brimmed with empathy and her voice rang with excitement.*

> *She noted that butterflies couldn't take flight when their wings were wet, a lesson she had learned through her observations and exploration of biology approximations. She called out to me, "Mommy, the butterfly's wings are wet! She can't fly like this." Her concern was so genuine; I was touched. She brought the butterfly inside the house and started crafting a little house—it was more like a room made inside a box. She used some napkins to make a bed, where she laid the butterfly, and she even added a piece of Oreo cookie!*

> *When I asked her what was she doing, she explained to me the butterfly needed to rest, and that's why she tried to make her a room: so she could wait until the rain passed to fly again when her wings had dried.*

Mastering Math, Language, and the Arts

Math and the Equation for Success

Mathematics play a fundamental role in the development of life skills for preschoolers, setting the stage for them to eventually become fully independent and thriving adults. Here are several reasons why mathematics is crucial during this formative period:

- **Problem-Solving Skills**: Mathematics encourages the development of critical problem-solving skills. From basic counting and simple arithmetic to more complex mathematical concepts, children learn to analyze situations, make decisions, and find solutions, which are essential life skills in various situations.

- **Logical Thinking**: Math instills logical thinking and reasoning abilities. Children learn to identify patterns, make connections, and think logically, which are essential for decision-making and problem-solving in daily life.

- **Numeracy**: Numeracy skills, which include understanding numbers and quantities, are vital in everyday tasks such as budgeting, shopping, and managing time. These foundational skills are crucial for financial independence and time management as adults.

- **Measurement and Units**: Understanding measurements and units is essential for daily tasks like cooking, DIY projects, and following instructions. Children learn about length, weight, volume, and time, which are used throughout their lives.

- **Spatial Awareness**: Mathematical concepts like shapes, sizes, and spatial relationships are important for understanding and interacting with the physical world. These skills are valuable for navigation, building, and design tasks.

- **Math as a Universal Language**: Math is a universal language that transcends cultural and linguistic barriers. Proficiency in mathematics allows individuals to communicate and work effectively in a globalized world.

- **Technology Literacy**: In the modern age, technology is intertwined with mathematics. Understanding mathematical principles is essential for using digital tools, computers, and various applications, which are critical for education and career success.

- **Preparation for Advanced Learning**: Proficiency in early math concepts paves the way for success in more advanced mathematics, science, and technology fields. It opens doors to a wide range of educational and career opportunities.

- **Financial Literacy**: Basic math skills are crucial for financial literacy. Children who understand mathematical concepts are better equipped to manage money, make informed financial decisions, and plan for their financial future as adults.

- **Independence and Self-Reliance**: Math empowers children to become independent and self-reliant. It provides them with the tools to calculate, measure, and solve problems on their own, reducing reliance on others for basic tasks.

- **Cognitive Development**: Engaging with mathematics enhances cognitive development, including memory, attention, and concentration, which are valuable life skills for learning and productivity.

In summary, mathematics cultivate problem-solving abilities, logical thinking, and numeracy skills that are essential for daily life, career success, and personal growth. By fostering a strong mathematical foundation during early childhood, children are better prepared to meet the challenges of adulthood and become self-reliant, capable individuals. The Montessori philosophy recognizes the importance of mathematics and thus offer a wide range of play-based activities designed to cultivate those maths-related life skills early on.

Each of the games and activities that you will find at the end of the book offers a practical approach to learning, combining recreation and education to support the development of crucial math and language skills in children. Depending on your child's interests and needs, you can incorporate them into your daily routines or assign dedicated learning sessions to them.

Language as a Foundation for Learning

Language is the primary medium through which knowledge is acquired. Proficient communication and language skills are essential for success in school and later academic pursuits. Children who can express themselves effectively are better equipped to understand and learn new concepts. To motivate and inspire parents to create a language-rich environment for children, here is a list of reasons why communication is so important:

- **Social Interaction**: Effective communication is vital for building and maintaining relationships. Through interactions with peers, teachers, and family, children develop social skills, empathy, and cooperation, which are essential for healthy social relationships in adulthood.

- **Emotional Expression**: Language provides a means for children to express their thoughts, feelings, and emotions. It helps them manage stress, resolve conflicts, and develop emotional intelligence, which is crucial for mental and emotional well-being as adults.

- **Problem-Solving and Critical Thinking**: Through language, children learn to articulate their thoughts and ideas, which is a crucial step in problem-solving and critical thinking. As they mature, they can use these skills to tackle complex issues and make informed decisions.

- **Reading and Writing Skills**: Literacy is a fundamental life skill. Language skills acquired during early childhood serve as the basis for reading and writing, enabling children to access and communicate information, which is essential for personal growth and career development.

- **Listening Skills**: Effective communication is a two-way street, and listening is as crucial as speaking. Children who develop strong listening skills are better equipped to comprehend instructions, learn from others, and collaborate effectively with colleagues as adults.

- **Conflict Resolution**: Language and communication enable children to express their concerns and resolve conflicts in a non-violent manner. These skills are invaluable for managing disputes in personal and professional relationships as adults.

- **Job Market Competency**: In the professional world, effective communication is often cited as a top skill that employers seek. Being able to convey ideas, collaborate with teams, and communicate clearly with clients and colleagues is crucial for career success.

- **Cultural Awareness and Diversity**: Language skills promote an understanding of different cultures, languages, and perspectives. This awareness is essential for navigating a diverse and interconnected global society.

- **Advocacy and Self-Expression**: Language empowers individuals to advocate for themselves, express their needs and desires, and stand up for their rights. This is critical for self-advocacy, leadership, and civic engagement in adulthood.

- **Creativity and Innovation**: Language fosters creativity by enabling individuals to express and explore ideas. It's a tool for innovation and problem-solving in various fields, from the arts to science and technology.

In addition to providing an extensive list of activities for language development at the end of the book, I would also like to remind parents of their role in shaping their young one's array of language and communication skills. During the first years of their lives, the vast majority of communicated information that the children receive will invariably come from their primary caregivers. The way in which this information is communicated is the model that they are likely to recreate when it is their turn to express their ideas, needs and feelings. This presents us, parents, with a great opportunity to step up our game as communicators, knowing just how important it is to set a good example for our kids. I invite parents to take this on, not as a stressful remorse-driven duty, but as an exciting opportunity to cultivate a skill that will improve many areas of their lives, as well as their children's, but will also provide a better communication blueprint that their children can use during their whole life.

Cultivating Artistic Expression and Creativity

Nurturing the artistic side of children is not just about encouraging them to create pretty pictures; it's about fostering essential skills and qualities that will benefit them throughout their lives.

Creativity encourages children to look at the world from different angles, explore various solutions, and think outside the box. These skills are fundamental for future problem-solving in any field. As children see their artistic skills grow and their creations take shape, their self-confidence receives a significant boost. This newfound confidence can spill over into other areas of life, prompting them to take on new challenges bravely. Moreover, arts and crafts often involve precise movements, which help improve fine motor skills; these are essential for tasks like writing or handling small objects.

Engaging in arts and crafts allows children to appreciate beauty in the world around them. This aesthetic awareness enriches their lives by helping them see and savor the beauty in every little thing. Furthermore, art exposes children to various cultures, traditions, and historical periods. They can explore the world through different artistic styles, gaining broader perspectives on human creativity and diversity.

Finally, art is a wonderful conduit through which your child can learn to channel their emotions and feelings into positive creativity. The more they use it for this purpose, the more they will grow confident and allow themselves to be vulnerable in a way that is not only accepted in society, but also celebrated. Known artists have usually started expressing their inner world through art at a very young age. You can give your child the gift of creating an environment where authentic artistic expression is safe and encouraged, setting the stage for whatever mature artistic endeavour they might decide to take on as young adults.

To conclude this chapter, let's hear some parents' testimonies about how their children have discovered and succeeded at new activities.

Tim shares his son's experience of discovering new artistic fields:

My son discovered a love for sculpting. His creativity knows no bounds as he sculpts intricate pieces with clay. For every piece of information coming his way during the day, it's like there is a little voice in his head, asking: Can I put this into clay? I'm grateful that my son has found a positive way to express his creative talents. The artistic creations he brings home never fails to amaze us.

Charles talks about his son's linguistic journey:

The language activities suggested by his Montessori program transformed my son into a language enthusiast. He eagerly shares new words and phrases he learns at school, and our dinner table conversations have become a delightful language exchange. He also recently opened up to the idea of learning other languages, which I initially took as a mix of excitement and anxiety as I, myself, only speak English and wondered if I was going to be up to the task of supporting him in his project. But thinking Montessori, I then remembered that my role is not to teach him a new language, but to shape an environment where that can happen, and provide the necessary tools and emotional support for him to do his own thing. That thought immediately turned my anxiety energy into excitement and I was eager to discuss with my son how we were going to set this up. He has been learning Japanese for the past four months now and is still very motivated without me doing anything to keep him on track with his program. I have no idea if he's going to speak the language fluently one day, but I know that through this, he is also learning to learn, a concept I first heard of through Montessori. Whatever the result is, seeing him take charge of his own study routine like this already exceeds what I thought my son was capable of, and makes me very confident for his success in the future.

CHAPTER 5:
A LIFETIME OF MONTESSORI PRINCIPLES

As children enter elementary school, Montessori principles continue to guide their educational experiences. The emphasis on individualized learning, mixed-age classrooms, and hands-on materials is extended. Students are encouraged to delve deeper into their areas of interest, collaborate with peers of different ages, and take on increased responsibilities within the learning environment. Montessori principles promote not only academic achievement but also social and emotional growth.

During the adolescent years, Montessori principles facilitate the transition from childhood to adulthood. Self-directed learning and autonomy are further developed, as students explore a broader range of subjects and have the opportunity to engage in internships, community service, and real-world projects. Mixed-age interactions continue to foster social development, and the focus shifts toward preparing teenagers for the responsibilities and challenges of adulthood.

Montessori principles remain relevant and applicable throughout adulthood. The concept of self-directed learning continues, in various forms, as adults pursue higher education, vocational training, or lifelong learning. The Montessori approach encourages individuals to take responsibility for their own growth, whether that involves personal development, career advancement, or continued education. This self-directed approach is invaluable in today's rapidly changing world, where adaptability and continuous learning are essential. Moreover, changes in technologies allow for more self-directed education opportunities than ever as a widening range of online courses, free lessons and tutorials are readily available at anytime, anywhere.

Even in the later stages of life, Montessori principles are beneficial. The emphasis on individuality, dignity, and the pursuit of interests can significantly enhance the quality of life for seniors. This stage encourages perpetual learning and the pursuit of hobbies, creative activities, and social engagement. Seniors can remain active, autonomous, and connected to their communities, fostering a sense of purpose and well-being.

Montessori principles are remarkably adaptable to every stage of human development, from birth to death. They provide a blueprint for nurturing individuality, independence, and a lifelong love of learning. By embracing these principles, individuals of all ages can engage in meaningful, self-directed activities that contribute to their overall well-being, personal growth, and success in the various stages of life. In this way, Montessori principles offer valuable guidance for a fulfilling and purposeful human journey.

Let's hear the testimony of Karl, father of a teen, who has successfully adopted the Montessori method throughout his child's life:

> As a father who embraced the Montessori principles, it's been quite the journey. We started this adventure when my lad, Jamie, was just a nipper. Our home became a place of exploration and curiosity. Jamie's love for music flourished, and we let him explore it freely. His room was like a mini music studio, with guitars and pianos.

Now that Jamie's a teenager, he's become a fiercely independent mu-
sician. He manages his music lessons and gigs himself. Montessori
taught him discipline and time management. It's brilliant to see him on
stage, confident and self-driven. Montessori isn't just about learning;
it's about fostering independence and passion. I couldn't be prouder of
the young man he's become, and I'm sure he will keep expressing his
passion for the rest of life.

Montessori Parenting Across the Ages

Now, let's look at how we can develop the skill of modifying our
parenting methods to suit our children's evolving requirements as
they navigate diverse phases of growth. This entails acknowledging
that what proves effective in promoting independence for a young
child may differ from what's necessary to steer a teenager toward
making responsible choices. Montessori principles serve as a ver-
satile framework that empowers us to tailor our strategies to each
child's distinct needs, embracing their changing interests, challenges, and aspirations, all while instilling a lifelong love for learning.

Supporting Creativity and Independence in All Stages of Childhood and beyond

Promoting creativity and independence throughout various stages of childhood involves recognizing that, regardless of their age,
every child has a unique creative spark waiting to be ignited. In
the early years, encouraging exploration and self-expression allows
creativity to blossom as toddlers interact with their surroundings.

As children progress through different developmental phases,
providing opportunities for independent decision-making and
self-guided learning empowers them to cultivate their individual
passions and interests. During adolescence, maintaining a secure
and nurturing environment enables teenagers to freely express
their creativity and develop a strong sense of self. Montessori principles are adaptable, ensuring every child's potential is celebrated.

To give you an idea of what the application of Montessori guidelines will evolve into as your child grows, let's take a quick look at what these principles would look like when applied to a teenager:

- **Respect for Autonomy**: Encouraging teenagers to take responsibility for their education. Providing choices in what they study and how they approach their learning. Allowing them to set their own goals and develop a sense of self-direction. This can include self-paced projects and exploration of personal interests.

- **Prepared Environment**: Creating a well-organized and aesthetically pleasing learning environment that is conducive to focus and exploration. This might include quiet study areas, access to resources, and materials tailored to their interests.

- **Individualized Learning**: Recognizing the diverse interests and abilities of teenagers. Tailoring learning experiences to meet individual needs and provide options for students to work at their own pace.

- **Real-World Applications**: Emphasizing the practical application of knowledge. Encouraging teenagers to engage in real-world projects, internships, and community service that connect classroom learning to their lives and the world around them.

- **Mixed-Age Groups**: Arranging opportunities for teenagers to collaborate with peers of different ages. This can encourage mentoring and leadership skills while promoting social and emotional growth.

- **Student-Led Discussions**: Promoting student-led discussions and dialogues. Encouraging teenagers to express their opinions, engage in debates, and develop their communication and critical thinking skills.

- **Freedom Within Limits**: While granting autonomy, establishing clear guidelines and boundaries that promote responsible decision-making. Encouraging teens to reflect on their choices and learn from mistakes.

- **Assessment and Feedback**: Moving away from traditional grading and focus on qualitative feedback. Helping teenagers assess their own work, set goals, and self-evaluate their progress.

- **Sustained Projects**: Encouraging long-term, self-directed projects that allow teenagers to dive deeply into topics of interest. These projects can develop research, time management, and problem-solving skills.

- **Practical Life Skills**: Including life skills education, such as cooking, budgeting, and time management, as part of the curriculum to prepare teenagers for independent living.

- **Technology Integration**: Leveraging technology as a tool for research, collaboration, and learning. Teaching digital literacy and responsible use of technology.

- **Encourage Creativity and Exploration**: Providing opportunities for artistic and creative expression, which can help teenagers explore their passions and develop innovative thinking.

- **Community Involvement**: Fostering a sense of social responsibility by involving teenagers in community service and civic engagement projects. This can help them develop empathy and leadership skills.

- **Emphasis on Mentorship**: Connecting teenagers with adult mentors, whether teachers, experts in their areas of interest, or professionals in the community, to guide and inspire them.

- **Open Communication**: Maintaining open lines of communication with teenagers, actively seeking their input and feedback on the educational experience. Encouraging them to discuss their goals and concerns.

- **Flexibility and Adaptability**: Being flexible and willing to adapt the learning environment and curriculum based on the changing needs and interests of teenagers.

Applying Montessori principles to a teenage learning environment can help foster independence, creativity and self-confidence while preparing them for the challenges and opportunities of adulthood. It's important to continually assess the effectiveness of these principles and make adjustments as needed to best support the development of each teenager.

Anna, a 67-year-old mother who opted for the Montessori method, shares her experience and the results she sees in her 28-year-old son:

> *Today, I see my son as a successful and self-driven adult. He continues to approach life with the same sense of wonder and self-assuredness that Montessori principles instilled in him during his formative years. He's grown into a calm and solution-oriented young man and is a lot wiser than I was at his age. He's a had a few bumps along the road of course, which is necessary for any human being to learn and grow, but I never lost confidence in his ability to deal with tough situations. I'm immensely grateful for the lasting impact Montessori has had on our lives. It helped shape not only my son's educational journey but also our shared memories of growth and discovery, and our bond between a mother and her child.*

A Legacy of Independence and Creativity

Montessori creates an environment where kids can be themselves, try new things, and enjoy the thrill of finding stuff out. It teaches them important life skills and gives them a solid foundation for the future. Montessori doesn't stop at school; it helps kids grow into responsible, creative, and curious individuals who see the world with wide eyes and a hunger for knowledge.

Encouraging Independence and Creativity in Future Generations

Encouraging children to develop autonomy and boosting their freedom of thought are pivotal in cultivating a generation characterized by critical thinking. When we motivate children to make their own choices, explore their passions and interests, and take control of their learning journey, we are facilitating the fundamental skills of autonomy and independence. These capabilities, in turn, prepare them to engage in critical thinking, where they can question, analyze, and evaluate information effectively.

Furthermore, promoting creativity and independence are naturally linked. Creative people often show an inclination to find new solutions to problems—a key element of critical thinking. By nurturing these qualities, we provide children with a powerful tool for addressing difficult issues with confidence and independence.

Encouraging autonomy and freedom not only benefits individual children but also contributes to the development of a society that values self-reliance and originality. It shapes a generation capable of confidently confronting future challenges while thinking critically, ultimately paving the way for a more promising and progressive future for all.

Montessori Legacy

The following story illustrates how the Montessori method can form a continuum throughout generations:

As a soon-to-be mom, I find myself reflecting on the incredible gift I received from my own parents—a Montessori upbringing. Their decision to embrace this educational philosophy has shaped me in profound ways, instilling a deep sense of independence, curiosity and basically wanting to learn everything. Now, as I prepare to welcome my own child into the world, I can't help but feel immensely grateful for the values and principles that were instilled in me.

Moreover, since I've experienced my third and fourth year at a regular school, I think I'm in a better position than most to appreciate the difference in education quality between the two systems. Not to throw dirt at anyone or anything here, but let's just say I've noticed quite the clash, both in motivation and joy in the classroom, which only makes me more thankful for having experienced the Montessori way during most of my time in school.

I wholeheartedly intend to pass on the torch of Montessori to my little one. I've seen firsthand how this approach nurtures critical thinking, self-motivation, and a strong sense of individuality. And above all that, the level of freedom we experience in a Montessori classroom simply feels good and more natural. I don't have the impression that it slowed me down in my development at all, on the contrary. It's a legacy I'm excited to continue, knowing that I'm offering my child the same opportunities for growth, exploration, and self-discovery that I was fortunate enough to experience.

So, to my parents, who did their best to raise me with Montessori, thank you. Your dedication to providing me with a Montessori education has given me not just a solid academic basis but also a set of life skills that I will now eagerly pass on to the next generation. Here's to the beautiful journey ahead, as I prepare to embrace parenthood with the same Montessori-inspired love and devotion.

Montessori Cultural and Social Studies: Global Citizens in the Making

Next, we'll delve into Montessori's unique approach to cultural and social studies, which shapes young learners into global citizens with a profound appreciation for inclusion and diversity and a thirst for understanding the world.

Montessori Perspective on Cultural and Social Studies

Montessori places a significant focus on nurturing social consciousness and emotional intelligence. By participating in activities that encourage cooperation, conflict resolution, and empathy, children gain an understanding of the significance of working together and building harmonious relationships in an ever more interconnected world.

Moreover, a Montessori education instills a sense of accountability toward environmental and global concerns. Children actively participate in discussions and projects that tackle subjects such as sustainability, cultural conservation, and social equity. This involvement empowers them to engage with and address critical issues, contributing to their development as informed and responsible global citizens.

Fostering Global Awareness and Cultural Appreciation

Nurturing global consciousness and cultivating an appreciation for various cultures in children is a rewarding journey that begins within the confines of our homes. An effective method involves exposing children to the multiple characteristics of world cultures through various channels. This may entail immersing them in literature that transports them to far-flung territories, viewing documentaries that showcase different ways of life, or embarking on family adventures to explore new cultures. These experiences serve as motivations, igniting your child's curiosity and widening their horizons.

Embracing diverse culinary traditions by incorporating international cuisines into family meals is another delightful avenue for cultural exploration. Cooking global dishes together not only awakens taste buds but also provides a medium for debating the cultural significance of ingredients and culinary traditions. It becomes a sensory and educational escapade that brings families closer to the heart of different cultures.

Jackson, father of a six-year-old boy, comments on his culinary adventures with his child:

I was up for a foodie adventure that promised a tasty dive into the world of Colombian cooking. So, with our aprons on and grins from ear to ear, my son and I geared up for a kitchen fiesta centered around the classic Colombian dish Bandeja Paisa. As we casually measured out ingredients like rice, beans, and plantains, I thought, why not sprinkle in some spice knowledge too? So, I casually told my son that these flavor enhancers, like cumin, paprika, and cilantro, weren't just about adding zing to our dish—they were like little storytellers from Colombia's vibrant culture and history. And with every pinch and dash of those spices, our kitchen filled up with a fragrant tale of Colombian traditions and the cozy vibes of family gatherings. All in all, this kitchen adventure wasn't just about mastering cooking; it was a reminder that food is a fantastic way to connect with different cultures and savor their unique stories.

A Holistic Approach: Fostering a Love for Learning Anything

Montessori principles, known for their effectiveness in education, reach beyond traditional boundaries, offering a framework for a holistic learning experience. From kids exploring nature to teens pursuing their interests and adults diving into new passions, Montessori empowers us to actively engage with the world, deepening our understanding of subjects that intrigue us.

Fostering Creativity, Independence, and a Love for Learning in All Environments

What's amazing about this method is its adaptability to unexpected areas of life. The Montessori method continues to exert a positive influence into adulthood, imparting enduring skills and values. It cultivates qualities like self-discipline, independence, and a passion for learning from an early age, which prove highly beneficial in professional settings as adults.

In the workplace, the ability to manage tasks, think critically, and efficiently use time, all originating from a Montessori education, becomes a significant advantage. Furthermore, the inclination to approach challenges with curiosity, adaptability, and a strong sense of commitment, nurtured during early education, can contribute to a successful and satisfying career. Thus, the Montessori method offers enduring support, fostering qualities that empower individuals to excel in the dynamic world of adulthood.

Business owners, constantly juggling with multiple situations and wearing many hats simultaneously will benefit greatly from a Montessori upbringing to help them keep all the balls in the air at all times. Employees showing independence, creativity and leadership will have an easier time working their way up the corporate ladder.

So whatever our professional situation is, the skills acquired through Montessori are universal and will always prove to be handy. And since every situation in Life provides an opportunity for learning and growing, this makes the investment in learning skills one of the best possible investment we can make. Reinforcing a child's innate love for learning from the earliest age provides immeasurable value, regardless of social and cultural upbringing. This is why I believe Montessori principles will never be outdated.

GUIDING A COMMUNITY OF MINDFUL PARENTS

Dear reader,

Our exploration of the Montessori Method is coming to a conclusion. I want to extend my sincere gratitude to you for having chosen this book to be your guide through the timeless philosophy of Montessori. It is my deepest wish that you now feel equipped with everything you need to navigate the captivating adventure of parenting with grace and joy. I strongly believe that the ideas and guidelines conveyed in this book can make a powerful and positive difference in shaping a healthy and mindful new generation of humans, ultimately making the world a far better place for everyone.

You can be of significant help to a community of curious parents, by sharing your kind and honest thoughts about this book on the Amazon page. By doing so, you will be supporting this book, as well as the thousands of parents and caregivers who will be looking for parental guidance on the Amazon bookstore for many years to come. So, from the bottom of my heart, and on behalf of every parent who may benefit from your precious words, I thank you.

Amazon US	*Amazon Canada*	*Amazon Australia*	*Amazon UK*

CONCLUSION: A LIFELONG MONTESSORI EXPEDITION

Throughout this book, the Montessori method has been presented in a largely positive light. However, it's important to emphasize that not everything parents attempt using this method will yield immediate results. Parenting is a journey filled with its share of challenges and triumphs. When embracing Montessori, you may encounter limitations that require adaptability, persistence, and creative problem-solving to tailor the method's principles to your family's unique needs.

But since the Montessori guidelines are aligned with the way children are naturally wired to learn, it promises to give parents and children the best chances at creating the most enjoyable and rewarding educational experience possible. So do your best to keep at it! And remember that all the treasures of the world are already present inside the child, and it is not required of us to force them out. We are simply allowing them to come out naturally by creating the best possible environment for our children.

Recapping Montessori Parenting

Montessori parenting stands out for its adaptability to the specific needs of each family. Rather than offering a specified, one-size-fits-all approach, it presents a flexible framework that effortlessly adapts to the diverse circumstances and dynamics intrinsic in different households. This capacity for adaptation is a defining strength of Montessori parenting.

What we've learned in this book is that the Montessori principles serve as a base guide that parents can tailor to suit their particular situations. Whether a family includes children of differing ages, a single parent navigating parenthood solo, or a bustling household, the Montessori principles can be adjusted to align with each family's unique needs. This adaptability empowers parents to create an environment that promotes independence, fosters creativity, and nurtures a love for learning while harmonizing with the family's unique rhythm.

This parenting journey isn't characterized by strict rules; instead, it is based on assuming core values and creatively incorporating them into daily family life. It acknowledges that each child is an individual with their own developmental pace and interests. Montessori parenting supports parents to adapt and evolve with their children, ensuring they provide the most enriching and nurturing environment for their development. Ultimately, it's this ability to adapt and cater to each family's unique needs that makes Montessori principles a lasting and invaluable guide on the lifelong journey of parenthood.

Throughout this book, we've been privileged to witness the transformative power of autonomy. From the tiny triumphs of toddlers learning to dress themselves to the awe-inspiring moments of teenagers making intelligent and reflexive choices, Montessori principles leave an unforgettable mark. These principles grant our children not just practical life skills but a profound sense of self-directed educational success

As we delve into Montessori education, we witness the deep impact it has on our children's lifelong adventure of self-discovery and growth. The empowerment it provides ignites a fondness for studying their interests with limitless curiosity. It's a rich and empowering undertaking that touches our hearts deeply as parents.

Inspiring Parents

As parents, we have a crucial role to play in our children's development, particularly when it comes to instilling important values that they will carry with them for life. It's not a passive role; we must actively participate in the process, fostering these values in our children through our actions and words.

Indeed, this journey is a lifelong responsibility, requiring abundant patience and empathy, and an endless openness to learning. We must be prepared to evolve and adapt at the same time as our children, always exploring novel ways to nurture their growth and development. As parents, our devotion to cultivating an environment where independence, creativity, and a profound love for learning flourish must persist. It's a constant odyssey, where the goal is not a static point but an ever-changing landscape of possibilities, guided by the principles of Montessori parenting.

The powerful testimonies shared throughout this book provides inspiration to embrace the Montessori principles as an ongoing dedication, a commitment that needs to be taken wholeheartedly. By adopting this approach to education and child-rearing, you will be able to create an environment that encourages your children to become lifelong learners, just like you. As Montessori parents, we do not simply teach our children—we learn alongside them, and that is a truly transformative experience.

Discovering Supportive Communities

Parenting makes you face a myriad of unpredictable situations, filled with both triumphs and challenges. Yet, you're never alone on this adventure. In today's digital age, an abundance of Montessori-inspired communities flourish on social media platforms like Facebook, X (formerly known as Twitter), and Instagram, offering a sanctuary of positivity, companionship, and practical help.

Stepping into one of these groups is like finding an oasis of understanding and encouragement. These communities emit warmth and acceptance, with seasoned Montessori parents generously sharing their wisdom, experience, and advice. It's a space where you can openly discuss your parenting hardships, knowing that kind-hearted fellow parents are ready to assist.

What sets Montessori groups apart is their solution-oriented approach. If you're grappling with a specific aspect of parenting, you're likely to find someone who has navigated a similar challenge and is eager to offer guidance. Whether it's sleepless nights or mealtime meltdowns, these communities provide comfort and actionable solutions.

Beyond troubleshooting, Montessori groups foster a profound sense of unity. They remind you that your parenting journey is shared with others who face similar problems and victories. Challenges become less daunting, and achievements are celebrated with genuine enthusiasm.

In the vast landscape of parenting resources, Montessori-inspired communities shine with optimism and mutual support. They showcase the transformative power of coming together, where parents of diverse backgrounds unite under the common banner of nurturing their children with love, patience, and the guiding light of the Montessori principles. Whether seeking guidance or offering your insights, remember that in the world of Montessori parenting, you're part of a compassionate and encouraging community that's here to motivate and inspire.

As we journey through this transformative strategy to education, let us remember that learning knows no limitations. It's a lifelong adventure, a voyage filled with endless curiosity, independence, and an insatiable appetite for knowledge. The path we've embarked upon, one of exploration, experimentation, and self-discovery, is not restricted to the classroom but extends into the very fabric of our lives. In our homes, we have the option of cultivating an atmosphere that fuels our children's natural wonder, self-reliance, and sheer joy in learning. So, let us continue to nurture their spirits, ignite their visions, and entrust them to soar as lifelong learners.

With each passing day, let us inspire our children to investigate, dream, and make their mark upon this world, leaving an indelible legacy of curiosity and infinite potential.

ACTIVITIES LIST

Notes On The Activities List

- This list is separated by age group in five main sections: 0 to 12 months, 12 to 24 months, 2 to 3, 3 to 4, and 4 to 5.

- Each main section is organized by activity type, such as *Arts and Crafts, Sensory and Motor Skills, Social and Emotional Development*, etc.

- Each activity in the list contains a brief description of the activity, a list of benefits, and suggested variations to keep the activity interesting for the child.

- The list is image-free as to include a maximum number of activities in the book. If a particular activity idea is not clear to you due to the absence of visual support, we invite you to look it up on the internet to get more information and images related to it.

- Some toys are sometimes mentioned, but not described in detail. (Example: Montessori Sound Cylinders) If you are not familiar with a particular object that is referred to, again we invite you to look it up on the internet, as there are plenty of images, videos, and text descriptions on these particular toys.

- Some activities will show up in more than one age group. Remember that although we kept the development stage of the child in mind when organizing this activities list, each child's development is different. You are invited to try activities that are not in the corresponding age group of your child if you feel like a certain activity would be fun and appropriate.

Have fun! Some activities will work right away, and some won't. But the way in which the activity is presented to the child and your personal enthusiasm about it will have a major influence on how the child adopts it. Be creative and flexible and do your best to adapt the activities to your child's unique situation.

0-12 Months

Sensory Exploration Activities

Sensory Treasure Basket

Description: Fill a basket with various textured objects (fabrics, soft toys, wooden items) for your baby to touch, explore, and grasp.

Benefits: Stimulates sensory development, encourages fine motor skills, and fosters curiosity.

Variations: Rotate the items regularly to maintain interest.

High-Contrast Black and White Cards

Description: Show your baby black and white pattern cards to enhance visual development.

Benefits: Enhances visual tracking and focus.

Variations: Introduce colorful cards as your baby grows.

Mirror Exploration

Description: Show your baby their reflection in a baby-safe mirror.

Benefits: Boosts self-awareness and visual tracking skills.

Variations: Use different types of mirrors, such as curved or fun-shaped ones.

Soft Fabric Scrap Play

Description: Provide an assortment of soft fabric scraps for your baby to touch, squeeze, and explore.

Benefits: Stimulates tactile exploration and sensory development.

Variations: Offer different types of fabric, such as silk, cotton, and fleece.

Nature Mobile

Description: Create a mobile with natural objects like pinecones, leaves, and feathers for your baby to observe and touch.

Benefits: Enhances visual tracking, nature appreciation, and sensory exploration.

Variations: Change the mobile components with the seasons.

Fruit and Vegetable Exploration

Description: Offer age-appropriate fruits and vegetables for your baby to touch, taste, and explore.

Benefits: Introduces new textures, flavors, and sensory experiences.

Variations: Explore a variety of fruits and vegetables.

Texture Sensory Bags

Description: Fill sealable plastic bags with various textures (rice, fabric, gel, water) for your baby to touch and squish.

Benefits: Encourages tactile exploration and sensory stimulation.

Variations: You can add colorful objects or foods, such as beads or sprinkles.

Texture Boards

Description: Create boards with various textured materials (sandpaper, fabric, velvet) for your baby to touch.

Benefits: Enhances tactile exploration and sensory development.

Variations: Use different textures and materials.

Texture Wall Art

Description: Hang textured art pieces at your baby's eye level for them to reach out and feel.

Benefits: Encourages sensory exploration and art appreciation.

Variations: Use different textured materials in the artwork.

Texture Walk

Description: Create a soft texture walkway using materials like fleece, sandpaper, or bubble wrap for your baby to explore while crawling.

Benefits: Enhances tactile and sensory awareness during movement.

Variations: Change the textures periodically.

Texture Books

Description: Create fabric or sensory texture books for your baby to explore through touch.

Benefits: Encourages sensory exploration and tactile discrimination.

Variations: Include different textures and materials in the books.

Motor Skill Development Activities

Sensory Board

Description: Create a sensory board with various textures and objects (e.g., buttons, key chains, zippers, ribbons, switches, locks, gears, etc.) for your baby to touch and manipulate.

Benefits: Enhances fine motor skills and sensory exploration.

Variations: Add or change textures and objects based on your baby's interests.

Tummy Time Play

Description: Place your baby on their tummy on a soft mat to encourage neck and upper body strength.

Benefits: Supports physical development and helps prevent flat head syndrome.

Variations: Add a mirror, toys, or interesting objects to engage your baby.

Baby Gym

Description: Set up a simple baby gym with hanging toys for your baby to reach.

Benefits: Enhances gross motor skills and hand-eye coordination.

Variations: Change the hanging toys to keep it interesting.

Soft Ball Rolling

Description: Roll a soft, lightweight ball towards your baby to encourage reaching and grasping.

Benefits: Develops hand-eye coordination and strengthens arm muscles.

Variations: Use balls of different sizes and textures.

Rattle Play

Description: Offer rattles with different sounds and textures for your baby to shake and explore.

Benefits: Enhances auditory and tactile sensory development.

Variations: Rotate the rattles to introduce new sounds.

Foot Painting

Description: Dip your baby's feet in baby-safe paint and let them make footprints on paper.

Benefits: Encourages foot and leg movement and introduces early art exploration.

Variations: Use different colors of washable, non-toxic paint.

Obstacle Course

Description: Create a safe, low obstacle course with pillows and soft objects for your baby to crawl or roll over.

Benefits: Enhances gross motor skills and spatial awareness.

Variations: Change the course layout periodically.

Baby Yoga

Description: Engage in gentle baby yoga poses and stretches with your baby, helping them move and stretch their limbs.

Benefits: Supports physical development, flexibility, and bonding.

Variations: Explore different baby yoga poses.

Cognitive Development Activities

High-Contrast Mobile

Description: Hang a black and white mobile above the crib to engage your baby's visual focus.

Benefits: Enhances visual tracking and concentration.

Variations: Introduce other visually stimulating mobiles.

Peek-a-Boo

Description: Play peek-a-boo with a soft cloth or blanket to teach object permanence.

Benefits: Enhances cognitive development and understanding of object permanence.

Variations: Try peek-a-boo with different objects.

Exploring Household Items

Description: Allow your baby to safely explore everyday objects like wooden spoons, cups, or scarves.

Benefits: Encourages curiosity, and object manipulation.

Variations: Introduce new household items for exploration.

Object Permanence Box

Description: Introduce an object permanence box with a small ball for your baby to practice dropping and retrieving.

Benefits: Develops the understanding of object permanence and fine motor skills.

Variations: Try boxes with different openings.

Early Math with Counting Toys

Description: Offer counting toys like stacking rings or nesting cups for your baby to explore and practice basic counting skills.

Benefits: Introduces early math concepts and fine motor development.

Variations: Explore toys with different shapes and numbers.

Object Exploration Tray

Description: Create a tray with various objects for your baby to examine, touch, and manipulate.

Benefits: Encourages curiosity, problem-solving, and exploration.

Variations: Rotate the objects regularly.

Shadow Play

Description: Use a flashlight to create simple shadow shapes on the wall for your baby to watch and explore.

Benefits: Enhances visual tracking, observation skills, and imagination.

Variations: Experiment with different shadow shapes.

Language Development Activities

Reading Aloud

Description: Read age-appropriate books to your baby, describing the pictures and engaging in conversation.

Benefits: Promotes language development, vocabulary, and bonding.

Variations: Explore different books and topics.

Singing Songs and Nursery Rhymes

Description: Sing lullabies and nursery rhymes to your baby, incorporating hand movements or actions.

Benefits: Encourages language development, rhythm, and social interaction.

Variations: Introduce new songs and actions.

Sound Imitation

Description: Make simple sounds like clapping, blowing kisses, or animal sounds and encourage your baby to imitate.

Benefits: Enhances sound recognition and early communication skills.

Variations: Introduce new sounds and actions.

Baby Sign Language

Description: Begin teaching simple baby sign language gestures like "more," "eat," "milk", or "all done."

Benefits: Facilitates early communication and reduces frustration.

Variations: Add more signs as your baby progresses.

Story Baskets

Description: Create story baskets with toys or objects related to a specific story and engage in storytelling with your baby.

Benefits: Promotes language comprehension, imagination, and storytelling skills.

Variations: Explore different story themes and objects.

Baby Babble Conversations

Description: Engage in "conversations" with your baby by responding to their coos, babbling, and vocalizations.

Benefits: Promotes early communication skills and bonding.

Variations: Mimic your baby's sounds and respond with enthusiasm.

Interactive Storytelling

Description: Tell interactive stories using simple props or puppets to engage your baby's attention and imagination.

Benefits: Enhances language development, creativity, and storytelling skills.

Variations: Create different story themes.

Social, Bonding, and Emotional Development Activities

Emotion Mirroring

Description: Mirror your baby's facial expressions and emotions to help them understand and express their feelings.

Benefits: Supports emotional development and empathy.

Variations: Try different facial expressions and emotions.

Family Photo Conversation

Description: Arrange photos of family members in front of your baby and describe each person, fostering a sense of family connection.

Benefits: Promotes language development, family recognition, and bonding.

Variations: Share stories or memories about each family member.

Social Interaction

Description: Encourage interactions with family members and peers through playdates and gentle social exposure.

Benefits: Develops social skills, communication, and emotional regulation.

Variations: Arrange playdates with different children.

Baby-Wearing

Description: Use a baby carrier or sling to keep your baby close while you go about your daily activities.

Benefits: Provides physical closeness, comfort, and security for your baby.

Variations: Explore different types of baby carriers.

Baby Massage

Description: Gently massage your baby using baby-safe oil, following gentle and soothing strokes.

Benefits: Promotes relaxation, enhances bonding, and stimulates sensory awareness.

Variations: Explore different massage techniques and rhythms.

Reading Together

Description: Choose age-appropriate books and read to your baby, making eye contact and using varying tones and expressions.

Benefits: Enhances language development, comprehension, and bonding.

Variations: Offer different books and themes.

Soft Toy Friends

Description: Provide soft and cuddly toys for your baby to interact with, cuddle, and bond with.

Benefits: Encourages attachment, emotional comfort, and sensory exploration.

Variations: Rotate soft toys to keep them interesting.

Calm and Quiet Time

Description: Create a calm and quiet environment for you and your baby, dimming lights, playing soft music, or using white noise.. Meditate or relax while your baby is present and observes you.

Benefits: Encourages relaxation, sensory awareness, and better sleep.

Variations: Experiment with different calming techniques.

Emotion Exploration

Description: Show pictures or drawings of different facial expressions to your baby and describe the associated emotions.

Benefits: Helps your baby recognize emotions and fosters empathy.

Variations: Use photos of family members displaying emotions.

Tickle Play

Description: Engage in gentle tickle play with your baby, using soft touches and playful sounds.

Benefits: Promotes bonding, laughter, and sensory awareness.

Variations: Tickle different parts of the body.

Mirror Dance

Description: Hold your baby in front of a full-length mirror and sway or dance together while making eye contact.

Benefits: Enhances body awareness, coordination, and bonding.

Variations: Play calming music during mirror time.

Practical Life Activities

Baby-Safe Cleaning Supplies

Description: Allow your baby to explore baby-safe cleaning supplies like a small broom or a cloth for gentle cleaning play.

Benefits: Fosters a sense of responsibility and involvement in daily tasks.

Variations: Clean different objects around the house.

Mealtime Observation

Description: Allow your baby to observe meal preparation and join you at the table during mealtime.

Benefits: Fosters a sense of inclusion, family bonding, and early exposure to food.

Variations: Offer baby-safe utensils to explore.

Laundry Basket Exploration

Description: Place your baby in a clean, empty laundry basket for them to sit in and explore.

Benefits: Encourages spatial awareness and offers a change of perspective.

Variations: Add soft toys or fabrics for sensory exploration, and change the location and height of the basket.

Stacking Cups

Description: Provide stacking cups for your baby to practice nesting and stacking.

Benefits: Enhances fine motor skills, coordination, and problem-solving.

Variations: Use cups of different sizes and materials. Also great during bath time once your baby can sit by himself.

Dressing Routine

Description: Involve your baby in the dressing routine by allowing them to hold items or put their arms through sleeves.

Benefits: Promotes independence and familiarity with daily routines.

Variations: Use clothing with large, easy-to-manipulate buttons or snaps.

Sock Matching

Description: Offer a pile of baby socks for your baby to practice matching by pairs.

Benefits: Introduces basic sorting skills and hand-eye coordination.

Variations: Use socks with different colors or patterns.

Feeding Independence

Description: Encourage self-feeding by providing age-appropriate finger foods and a safe feeding environment.

Benefits: Promotes independence, fine motor skills, and a positive relationship with food.

Variations: Offer a variety of healthy finger foods.

Gentle Toothbrush Play

Description: Offer a soft baby toothbrush for your baby to explore by touching their gums or practicing brushing.

Benefits: Introduces oral hygiene awareness and sensory exploration.

Variations: Use a baby-friendly toothpaste if desired.

Outdoor and Nature Activities

Nature Walks

Description: Take your baby on gentle nature walks to explore the outdoors and observe natural surroundings.

Benefits: Stimulates sensory exploration, connection with nature, and fresh air exposure.

Variations: Visit different natural settings.

Outdoor Blanket Time

Description: Place a soft blanket on the grass and allow your baby to experience outdoor play in a controlled environment.

Benefits: Introduces outdoor sensory experiences and fresh air exposure.

Variations: Bring along outdoor-safe toys.

Gentle Playground Exploration

Description: Visit baby-friendly playgrounds with simple equipment for exploration.

Benefits: Supports gross motor development and social exposure.

Variations: Choose playgrounds suitable for young babies.

Leaf and Flower Sensory Exploration

Description: Collect leaves and flowers during nature walks and let your baby touch, smell and explore them.

Benefits: Enhances sensory exploration, nature appreciation, and outdoor bonding.

Variations: Discover different types of leaves and flowers, in different settings such as forests, gardens, parks, etc.

Outdoor Picnics

Description: Enjoy outdoor picnics with age-appropriate finger foods, encouraging sensory exploration and outdoor dining.

Benefits: Fosters a love for nature, family bonding, and sensory experiences.

Variations: Picnic in various outdoor settings.

Gentle Water Splashing

Description: Fill a shallow container with a small amount of water for your baby to explore by splashing gently.

Benefits: Introduces water sensory experiences and hand-eye coordination.

Variations: Use different containers and outdoor settings.

Sand Play

Description: Provide a baby-friendly sandpit for your baby to touch and explore sand using safe sand toys.

Benefits: Stimulates tactile exploration, creativity, and outdoor play.

Variations: Add water to the sand to enhance tactile exploration.

Music and Sound Activities

Musical Shakers

Description: Fill small bottles with various materials (rice, beans, bells) for your baby to shake and hear different sounds.

Benefits: Enhances auditory exploration and sound discrimination. Encourages rhythm and coordination.

Variations: Experiment with different fillings and container sizes for varied sounds.

Musical Sing-Along

Description: Sing simple songs to your baby and use instruments like a small xylophone or handbells for added musical exploration.

Benefits: Enhances auditory perception, language development, and appreciation for music.

Variations: Explore various songs and instruments.

Instrument Exploration

Description: Provide a variety of musical instruments for your baby to touch, explore, and create sounds.

Benefits: Enhances auditory exploration, rhythm, and creativity.

Variations: Offer a wide range of instruments to experiment with.

Storytelling with Sound Effects

Description: Tell stories to your baby using sound effects or simple musical instruments to create an interactive narrative.

Benefits: Stimulates imagination, language development, and engagement.

Variations: Create unique stories with different themes.

Gentle Lullabies

Description: Sing lullabies to your baby at naptime and bedtime to establish a calming bedtime routine.

Benefits: Encourages relaxation, sleep routine development, and bonding.

Variations: Choose soothing lullabies and melodies.

Rhyme and Rhythm Books

Description: Read rhythmic and rhyming books to your baby, emphasizing the cadence and rhythm of the words.

Benefits: Enhances language development, rhythm perception, and phonemic awareness.

Variations: Explore different rhyming books.

Nature's Symphony

Description: Put yourself and your baby in an environment rich with sounds, without any distractions such as toys, and listen to the sounds of nature like wind rustling through trees, waves crashing, or rain falling.

Benefits: Encourages auditory exploration, relaxation, and appreciation for the natural world.

Variations: Explore different natural soundscapes.

12-24 Months

Fine Motor Skill Development Activities

Stacking Cups

Description: Provide a set of stacking cups for your toddler to stack, nest, and explore.

Benefits: Enhances fine motor skills, hand-eye coordination, and spatial awareness.

Variations: Experiment with cups of different sizes and materials.

Pegging Activities

Description: Offer a pegboard with large pegs for your toddler to insert and remove, developing fine motor control and hand strength.

Benefits: Promotes hand-eye coordination, problem-solving, and patience.

Variations: Use pegs of various shapes and colors.

Lacing and Threading

Description: Provide lacing cards and strings or shoelaces for your toddler to practice threading.

Benefits: Develops fine motor skills, hand-eye coordination, and concentration.

Variations: Explore different lacing card designs.

Pouring and Transferring

Description: Offer small containers and objects for your toddler to practice pouring and transferring items between containers.

Benefits: Enhances fine motor control, hand strength, and concentration.

Variations: Use different objects and container sizes.

Buttoning and Snapping

Description: Introduce clothing items with buttons or snaps, allowing your toddler to practice fastening and unfastening.

Benefits: Develops fine motor skills, finger dexterity, and dressing independence.

Variations: Use clothes with different fasteners.

Clay Sculpting

Description: Provide child-safe clay or playdough and encourage the child to sculpt objects or shapes.

Benefits: Develops fine motor skills, creativity, and a sense of 3D form.

Variations: Use different types of clay or introduce tools for sculpting.

Sensory Exploration Activities

Sensory Bin Exploration

Description: Fill a shallow container with materials like rice, sand, or beans for tactile exploration.

Benefits: Enhances sensory awareness, fine motor skills, and imaginative play.

Variations: Change the materials for new textures and experiences.

Nature Scavenger Hunt

Description: Create a list of natural items with images for your toddler to find during outdoor walks, promoting observation skills and a love for nature.

Benefits: Encourages outdoor exploration, connection with nature, and vocabulary development.

Variations: Adjust the list based on the season or location.

Finger Painting

Description: Allow your toddler to finger paint with non-toxic, washable paint on large paper.

Benefits: Promotes creativity, fine motor skills, and sensory exploration.

Variations: Use various colors and different painting tools or feet instead of hands.

Sensory Board

Description: Create a sensory board with various textures and objects (e.g., buttons, key chains, zippers, ribbons, switches, locks, gears, etc.) for your baby to touch and manipulate.

Benefits: Enhances fine motor skills and sensory exploration.

Variations: Add or change textures and objects based on your child's interests.

Nature's Sensory Bin

Description: Create a sensory bin with natural materials like sand, pinecones, and shells for tactile exploration.

Benefits: Stimulates sensory exploration, fine motor skills, and creativity.

Variations: Use different natural materials.

Practical Life Activities

Dressing Independence

Description: Encourage your toddler to dress themselves with simple clothing items like pants, shirts with large buttons, rain boots, hat, etc.

Benefits: Promotes independence, fine motor skills, and self-confidence.

Variations: Gradually introduce more complex clothing items.

Meal Preparation

Description: Involve your toddler in simple meal preparation tasks like washing vegetables, mixing, or spreading butter on bread,

Benefits: Fosters independence, fine motor skills, and an appreciation for cooking.

Variations: Try age-appropriate kitchen tasks.

Planting Seeds

Description: Plant seeds or seedlings with your toddler in a garden or indoor pot, allowing them to care for the plants.

Benefits: Nurtures a connection with nature, responsibility, and patience.

Variations: Choose different types of plants.

Feeding Pets

Description: Encourage your toddler to help feed and care for family pets, fostering a sense of responsibility and empathy.

Benefits: Teaches responsibility, empathy, and a love for animals.

Variations: Involve your toddler in pet grooming tasks.

Dressing and Undressing Dolls

Description: Provide dolls or stuffed animals with removable clothing and demonstrate how to dress and undress them.

Benefits: Encourages independence, fine motor skills, and self-help skills.

Variations: Use different dolls or introduce more complex clothing items.

Helping with Daily Chores

Description: Involve your child in simple daily chores like setting the table or putting away toys.

Benefits: Fosters a sense of contribution, responsibility, and co-operation.

Variations: Introduce new chores as your child grows.

Outdoor and Nature Activities

Water Painting

Description: Offer a water container with brushes of different sizes for your toddler to paint on a concrete wall.

Benefits: Stimulates creativity, hand-eye coordination, and relaxation.

Variations: Use colored water or different brushes.

Nature Art with Leaves

Description: Collect leaves during outdoor walks and use them to create art by gluing them onto paper.

Benefits: Enhances creativity, fine motor skills, and a connection with nature.

Variations: Create leaf rubbings or leaf collages.

Nature Scavenger Hunt

Description: Create a list of natural items (e.g., pinecones, acorns, feathers) for your toddler to find during outdoor adventures.

Benefits: Promotes observation skills, nature appreciation, and excitement for exploration.

Variations: Customize scavenger hunts for different outdoor locations.

Outdoor Picnics

Description: Enjoy outdoor picnics with toddler-friendly finger foods, encouraging outdoor dining and exploration.

Benefits: Fosters a love for nature, family bonding, and sensory experiences.

Variations: Change the picnic location.

Outdoor Obstacle Course

Description: Set up a safe, age-appropriate obstacle course with items like cones, hoops, and tunnels for your toddler to navigate.

Benefits: Enhances gross motor skills, coordination, and physical confidence.

Variations: Change the course layout regularly.

Bird Watching

Description: Set up bird feeders and binoculars for your toddler to observe and identify birds in your backyard or at a local park.

Benefits: Enhances observation skills, bird identification, and nature appreciation.

Variations: Learn about different bird species.

Nature Collections

Description: Go on nature walks with your toddler to collect and document interesting natural items like leaves, rocks, or shells.

Benefits: Fosters a connection with nature, observation skills, and an appreciation for the outdoors.

Variations: Create themed nature collections.

Gardening Together

Description: Involve your toddler in gardening tasks like planting, watering, and weeding in a garden or plant pots.

Benefits: Nurtures a love for gardening, responsibility, and sensory exploration.

Variations: Choose different plants or vegetables to grow.

Rock Painting

Description: Gather smooth rocks and paint them with your toddler, encouraging creativity and nature-themed designs.

Benefits: Enhances artistic expression, fine motor skills, and a connection with nature.

Variations: Paint rocks with different patterns or colors.

Bug and Insect Exploration

Description: While outdoors, observe and discuss insects and bugs you encounter with your toddler, encouraging curiosity and respect for nature.

Benefits: Fosters observation skills, empathy for insects, and a love for the outdoors.

Variations: Learn about different insect species.

Butterfly Watching

Description: Learn about butterflies and observe them in gardens or parks, discussing their colors and behavior with your toddler.

Benefits: Encourages observation skills, insect knowledge, and appreciation for nature's beauty.

Variations: Explore different butterfly species.

Outdoor Yoga and Relaxation

Description: Practice simple outdoor yoga and relaxation exercises with your toddler, connecting with nature and promoting mindfulness.

Benefits: Enhances body awareness, relaxation, and a connection with the natural environment.

Variations: Explore different yoga poses and relaxation techniques.

Music and Sound Activities

Birdsong Symphonies

Description: Listen to birdsongs and try to mimic them using your voices or simple instruments like whistles.

Benefits: Encourages auditory exploration, creativity, and an appreciation for birds.

Variations: Learn about different birds and their songs.

Musical Instrument Exploration

Description: Provide a variety of musical instruments for your toddler to explore and play, encouraging auditory exploration and creativity.

Benefits: Enhances rhythm, auditory discrimination, and fine motor skills.

Variations: Offer different musical instruments to experiment with.

Singing and Movement

Description: Sing songs with your toddler while incorporating movements like clapping, stomping, or dancing.

Benefits: Promotes language development, rhythm perception, and physical coordination.

Variations: Explore different songs and movements.

Musical Storytelling

Description: Create musical stories by narrating simple tales with background music or sound effects.

Benefits: Fosters imagination, language development, and music appreciation.

Variations: Create stories with different themes.

Nature's Symphony

Description: Listen to the sounds of nature like wind rustling through trees, waves crashing, or rain falling.

Benefits: Encourages auditory exploration, relaxation, and appreciation for the natural world.

Variations: Explore different natural soundscapes.

Sound Exploration with Natural Objects

Description: Collect natural objects like pinecones, leaves, or rocks and experiment with the sounds they make when tapped, shaken, or scraped.

Benefits: Enhances auditory perception, creativity, and exploration.

Variations: Discover different natural materials and their sounds.

Nature-Inspired Songs

Description: Sing songs related to nature and incorporate outdoor elements into your singing, like using leaves as makeshift instruments.

Benefits: Promotes language development, bonding, and a connection with nature.

Variations: Explore songs from different cultures or traditions.

Language and Communication Activities

Nature Vocabulary Cards

Description: Create vocabulary cards with pictures of natural objects (e.g., trees, animals, flowers) to expand your toddler's vocabulary.

Benefits: Enhances language development, word recognition, and nature appreciation.

Variations: Use cards with different themes.

Reading Aloud

Description: Read age-appropriate books aloud to your toddler, discussing the story and pictures to promote language development and comprehension.

Benefits: Enhances vocabulary, comprehension, and bonding.

Variations: Explore different books and themes.

Outdoor Storytelling

Description: Tell nature-themed stories or create imaginative tales while enjoying outdoor settings with your toddler.

Benefits: Fosters imagination, language development, and a connection with nature.

Variations: Invent stories related to different outdoor locations.

Conversation with Nature

Description: Encourage your toddler to engage in conversations with natural elements during outdoor walks, like talking to a tree or a bird.

Benefits: Fosters imagination, language development, and a connection with nature.

Variations: Explore different aspects of nature to converse with.

Storytelling with Puppets

Description: Use hand puppets or stuffed animals to tell stories and encourage the child to participate in storytelling.

Benefits: Fosters language development, creativity, and imagination.

Variations: Create different story scenarios and characters.

Social, Bonding, and Emotional Development Activities

Outdoor Group Play

Description: Organize outdoor playdates with other toddlers to promote social interaction, sharing, and cooperation.

Benefits: Enhances social skills, communication, and friendship building.

Variations: Change activities and people to play with.

Nature Art Exhibition

Description: Organize a small outdoor art exhibition with your toddler's nature-inspired artwork for family and friends to admire.

Benefits: Fosters a sense of pride, confidence, and creativity.

Variations: Include other children's artwork as well.

Community Visits

Description: Plan visits to places like the library, fire station, or farmer's market to explore the community.

Benefits: Encourages social interaction, awareness of the world, and curiosity about the community.

Variations: Explore different community locations and discuss what they offer.

Indoor Fort Building

Description: Collaborate with your child to build indoor forts using blankets and cushions. Discuss cooperation and teamwork.

Benefits: Promotes teamwork, creativity, and imaginative play.

Variations: Experiment with different fort designs and uses.

Mindful Breathing with a Hug

Description: Practice mindful breathing together with your child, using a soft, comforting object to hug during deep breaths.

Benefits: Teaches emotional regulation, relaxation, and bonding.

Variations: Use a favorite stuffed animal or a cozy blanket.

Cognitive Development Activities

Color Mixing with Watercolors

Description: Allow the child to experiment with watercolors and explore color mixing.

Benefits: Enhances creativity, fine motor skills, and an understanding of color theory.

Variations: Experiment with different color combinations and painting techniques.

Memory Games

Description: Play simple memory games using cards with matching images and encourage the child to find the pairs.

Benefits: Enhances memory, concentration, and cognitive skills.

Variations: Increase the number of cards or introduce more complex images as the child's memory improves.

Block Stacking

Description: Offer a set of wooden or foam blocks and encourage your child to build towers and structures.

Benefits: Develops spatial awareness, problem-solving skills, and fine motor skills.

Variations: Introduce different block shapes and sizes.

Hand-Eye Coordination with Ball Play

Description: Engage in ball play, encouraging your child to catch, throw, and aim at targets.

Benefits: Enhances hand-eye coordination, motor skills, and spatial awareness.

Variations: Use different types of balls, set up targets, or try different throwing games.

Puzzles

Description: Offer age-appropriate puzzles with large pieces. Encourage your child to complete the puzzle, which aids in problem-solving and cognitive development.

Benefits: Enhances spatial awareness, hand-eye coordination, and logical thinking.

Variations: Choose puzzles with different themes or levels of complexity.

2 to 3 years

Practical Life Skills

Pouring Water

Description: Provide a small pitcher and a glass for your toddler to pour water into the glass.

Benefits: Develops hand-eye coordination, fine motor skills, and independence.

Variations: Use colored water for added visual appeal or containers of different sizes and shapes.

Dressing Skills

Description: Encourage your toddler to dress and undress independently, starting with simple items like shirts, socks, hats, weather boots.

Benefits: Fosters self-reliance, fine motor skills, and a sense of accomplishment.

Variation: Practice different types of clothing.

Table Setting

Description: Teach your toddler to set the table, placing utensils, plates, and cups in their proper places.

Benefits: Promotes orderliness, sequencing, and responsibility.

Variations: Use placemats with illustrations of where items should go.

Food Preparation

Description: Involve your toddler in age-appropriate food preparation tasks, like spreading butter on bread, slicing soft fruits.

Benefits: Enhances coordination, confidence, and a connection to food.

Variations: Explore different foods and preparation methods.

Plant Care

Description: Allow your toddler to care for a small potted plant by watering it and observing its growth.

Benefits: Nurtures responsibility, understanding of plant life, and a connection with nature.

Variations: Plant different types of plants.

Cleanup Practice

Description: Engage your toddler in daily cleanup activities like sweeping, dusting, or folding laundry to develop practical life skills.

Benefits: Builds independence, responsibility, and fine motor skills.

Variations: Explore various household tasks.

Cooking Together

Description: Involve your toddler in simple cooking activities like mixing, pouring, or rolling dough.

Benefits: Enhances culinary skills, understanding of food, and creativity.

Variations: Cook different recipes together.

Nature Cleanup

Description: Teach your toddler to clean up natural materials like leaves or sticks after outdoor play.

Benefits: Fosters responsibility, environmental awareness, and tidiness.

Variations: Clean up different outdoor play areas.

Buttoning and Snapping

Description: Introduce clothing items with buttons or snaps, allowing your toddler to practice fastening and unfastening.

Benefits: Develops fine motor skills, finger dexterity, and dressing independence.

Variations: Use clothes with different fasteners.

Cognitive Development Activities

Memory Card Games

Description: Play simple memory card games with matching pairs. This boosts memory skills and concentration.

Benefits: Enhances memory skills and concentration.

Variations: Add a scoring system with goals to reach.

Building Blocks Match

Description: Build simple structures with blocks and challenge your child to create the same structure.

Benefits: Enhances spatial awareness, problem-solving skills and concentration.

Variations: Vary the complexity of the structures to match the child's abilities.

Shape and Letter Tracing

Description: Introduce basic shape and letter tracing activities to prepare for writing and reading. Use large, easy-to-hold writing tools and guide your child's hand in tracing shapes and letters.

Benefits: Develops hand-eye coordination, fine-motor skills and concentration.

Variations: Use more complex shapes like animals or fruits and vegetables as the child progresses.

Puzzle play

Description: Provide age-appropriate puzzles with large, simple pieces.

Benefits: Develops observation, problem-solving and fine-mortor skills.

Variations: Use more complex puzzles as the child progresses.

Building a Fort with Blankets

Description: Use blankets or sheets to create a fort. Encourage the child to help build and arrange the blankets.

Benefits: Stimulates creativity, spatial awareness and promotes cooperation and teamwork.

Variations: Add lighting elements or make a picnic inside the fort.

Sensory and Motor Skills Activities

Nature Sensory Walk

Description: Take a sensory nature walk, encouraging your toddler to touch leaves, smell flowers, and listen to the sounds of nature.

Benefits: Enhances sensory awareness, nature appreciation, and outdoor exploration.

Variations: Explore different outdoor environments.

Sensory Board

Description: Create a sensory board with various textured materials and safe interactive hardware pieces like locks, chains, gears, switches, etc.

Benefits: Develops tactile discrimination, sensory awareness, and fine motor skills.

Variations: Include different textures and materials.

Water and Sand Play

Description: Provide a water table or sandbox for children to explore and experiment with water, sand, and various tools.

Benefits: Enhances sensory exploration, fine motor skills, and creativity.

Variations: Add toys, molds, or natural elements like shells or pebbles.

Natural Playdough

Description: Make natural playdough using ingredients like flour, salt, and natural dyes for creative play.

Benefits: Enhances fine motor skills, creativity, and sensory exploration.

Variations: Experiment with scents and colors.

Scented Sensory Bins

Description: Fill sensory bins with scented materials like dried herbs, flowers, car freshners, essential oils on pieces of cloth, for olfactory exploration.

Benefits: Stimulates the sense of smell, sensory awareness, and relaxation.

Variations: Use different scents and materials.

Water Pouring with Precision

Description: Provide a pitcher and two glasses for your toddler to pour water accurately from one glass to another.

Benefits: Develops hand-eye coordination, fine motor skills, and concentration.

Variations: Use different-sized containers.

Obstacle Course

Description: Set up an indoor or outdoor obstacle course using cushions, tunnels, and cones, promoting physical activity and coordination.

Benefits: Enhances gross motor skills, balance, and spatial awareness.

Variations: Change the course layout for variety.

Language and Communication Activities

Montessori Sandpaper Letters

Description: Introduce Montessori sandpaper letters to help children learn letter shapes by touch. Encourage them to trace the letters.

Benefits: Enhances letter recognition, tactile exploration, and pre-reading skills.

Variations: Progress to more advanced letter materials.

DIY Story Cubes

Description: Create story cubes with images of different nature elements. Roll the cubes and create stories based on the images.

Benefits: Enhances storytelling skills, vocabulary development, and creativity.

Variations: Make story cubes with various themes or settings.

Storytime

Description: Read age-appropriate books to your toddler, discussing the story and asking open-ended questions.

Benefits: Promotes language development, vocabulary, and a love for reading.

Variations: Explore different genres of books.

Nature Vocabulary Cards

Description: Create vocabulary cards with pictures of natural objects (e.g., animals, plants) to expand your toddler's vocabulary.

Benefits: Enhances language development, word recognition, and nature appreciation.

Variations: Use cards with different themes.

Outdoor Storytelling

Description: Practice storytelling outdoors, taking turns to create imaginative tales based on the natural surroundings, fostering imagination and language development.

Benefits: Encourages creativity, language development, and a connection with nature.

Variations: Explore different storytelling themes.

Math and Numeracy Activities

Montessori Number Cards

Description: Introduce Montessori number cards with quantities represented by dots. Children can match the number to the quantity.

Benefits: Enhances number recognition, counting, and fine motor skills.

Variations: Progress to more advanced number cards.

Number Bean Sorting

Description: Provide children with a variety of beans or small objects to sort into containers based on numbers (e.g., place 3 beans in one container).

Benefits: Enhances counting, sorting, and fine motor skills.

Variations: Increase the number range as children develop their skills.

Nature Math

Description: Use natural materials like sticks, pebbles, or acorns for math activities. Children can practice counting, adding, or making simple patterns.

Benefits: Fosters numeracy, problem-solving, and a connection to nature.

Variations: Explore different math concepts and challenges.

Number Line Hopscotch

Description: Create a number line on the ground with chalk and play hopscotch. Children can jump on the numbers while counting.

Benefits: Promotes number recognition, counting skills, and physical activity.

Variations: Use hopscotch for basic addition or subtraction.

DIY Abacus

Description: Help children create a simple abacus using beads and string. They can use it to practice counting and simple addition.

Benefits: Promotes counting skills, understanding of quantities, and fine motor skills.

Variations: Experiment with different colors and sizes of beads.

Science and Nature Exploration

Nature Treasure Hunt

Description: Go on nature treasure hunts, searching for specific natural items (e.g., pinecones, rocks) and naming them.

Benefits: Improves vocabulary, observation skills, and outdoor exploration.

Variations: Focus on different categories of items.

Seed Planting

Description: Plant seeds in pots or a small garden, allowing your toddler to observe and care for the growing plants.

Benefits: Nurtures a love for gardening, responsibility, and understanding of plant life.

Variations: Plant different types of seeds.

Weather Observation Cards

Description: Discuss and observe different weather conditions with your toddler, and determine together which of the Weather Cards describes best the current conditions..

Benefits: Introduces weather concepts, observation skills, and scientific exploration.

Variations: Explore different weather patterns.

Bug Hotel Creation

Description: Build a bug hotel together using natural materials like sticks, leaves, and pinecones, providing shelter for insects in your garden, promoting empathy for insects and environmental awareness.

Benefits: Nurtures empathy for insects, environmental awareness, and construction skills.

Variations: Experiment with bug hotel designs.

Animal Tracks

Description: Search for animal tracks in mud or sand during nature walks, identifying the animals responsible.

Benefits: Enhances tracking skills, nature awareness, and understanding of animal behavior.

Variations: Explore different animal tracks.

Nature Collections

Description: Go on nature walks with your toddler to collect and document interesting natural items like leaves, rocks, or shells.

Benefits: Fosters a connection with nature, observation skills, and an appreciation for the outdoors.

Variations: Create themed nature collections.

Outdoor Yoga and Relaxation

Description: Practice simple outdoor yoga and relaxation exercises with your toddler, connecting with nature and promoting mindfulness, enhancing body awareness, relaxation, and a connection with the natural environment.

Benefits: Enhances body awareness, relaxation, and a connection with the natural world.

Variations: Explore different yoga poses and relaxation techniques.

Planting a Butterfly Garden

Description: Plant butterfly-friendly flowers and plants in your garden or pots, learning about plant care and attracting butterflies, nurturing a love for gardening and responsibility.

Benefits: Nurtures a love for gardening, responsibility, and awareness of the ecosystem.

Variations: Choose different butterfly-attracting plants.

DIY Science Experiments

Description: Conduct simple science experiments, like creating a volcano with baking soda and vinegar or making a vortex taping together two plastic bottles half-filled with coloured water.

Benefits: Enhances curiosity, problem-solving, and basic scientific understanding.

Variations: Explore a variety of age-appropriate science experiments.

DIY Mini Greenhouse

Description: Create a small greenhouse together with clear plastic containers to grow seeds or plants indoors.

Benefits: Teaches plant growth, responsibility, and an understanding of ecosystems.

Variations: Experiment with different types of seeds or plants.

Arts and Crafts Activities

Leaf Rubbings

Description: Collect leaves of different shapes and textures and create leaf rubbings using crayons and paper, fostering creativity and exploration.

Benefits: Enhances fine motor skills, texture exploration, and appreciation for leaf diversity.

Variations: Explore leaves with various colors and sizes.

Nature Shadow Art

Description: Experiment with creating art using natural objects and sunlight or spotlight to cast shadows, promoting artistic expression and creativity.

Benefits: Enhances fine motor skills, creativity, and understanding of light and shadow.

Variations: Explore different objects and angles for shadow art.

Nature Collages

Description: Collect natural materials like leaves, petals, and twigs to create collages with glue and paper.

Benefits: Fosters creativity, fine motor skills, and an appreciation for nature's textures.

Variations: Create themed collages.

Recycled Art Projects

Description: Provide a collection of recyclable materials (e.g., cardboard, bottle caps) for children to create sculptures, collages, or functional art.

Benefits: Fosters creativity, fine motor skills, and environmental awareness.

Variations: Explore different recycled materials and art projects.

Bead Stringing

Description: Provide large beads and strings for children to practice threading. They can create necklaces or bracelets.

Benefits: Fosters fine motor skills, hand-eye coordination, and concentration.

Variations: Use beads of different sizes or introduce patterns.

Paper Collage

Description: Provide colored paper and glue. Children can tear and glue the paper to create colorful collages.

Benefits: Enhances creativity, fine motor skills, and color recognition.

Variations: Explore different collage themes.

Nature Printing

Description: Collect leaves, flowers, pinecones, or tree bark. Dip them in paint and use them to create prints on paper or fabric.

Benefits: Fosters creativity, fine motor skills, and an appreciation for nature.

Variations: Experiment with different natural materials and printing surfaces.

Music and Sound Activities

Montessori Sound Cylinders

Description: Introduce Montessori sound cylinders with pairs of containers that make matching sounds. Encourage children to match the sounds.

Benefits: Enhances auditory discrimination, sound recognition, and concentration.

Variations: Progress to more complex sound cylinders.

Homemade Shakers

Description: Help children create their own shakers using small containers filled with rice, beans, or pasta. Encourage them to shake and make music.

Benefits: Fosters creativity, fine motor skills, and an understanding of cause and effect.

Variations: Experiment with different fillings for the shakers or decorate them.

Outdoor Drum Circle

Description: Arrange an outdoor drum circle with simple hand drums, buckets, or pans. Let children explore rhythm and make music together.

Benefits: Promotes rhythm awareness, social interaction, and physical activity.

Variations: Use various percussion instruments or introduce rhythmic patterns.

Nature Sound Jars

Description: Create sound jars by filling clear containers with natural materials like stones, shells, or pinecones. Children can shake and compare the sounds.

Benefits: Enhances auditory discrimination, sensory exploration, and language development.

Variations: Use different natural materials for the sound jars.

Music with Everyday Objects

Description: Encourage children to make music using everyday objects like pots, pans, wooden spoons, or empty plastic bottles.

Benefits: Promotes creativity, fine motor skills, and imaginative play.

Variations: Explore different objects and create "music ensembles."

DIY Xylophone

Description: Help children create a simple xylophone using glasses or bottles filled with varying amounts of water. They can experiment with different notes.

Benefits: Fosters an understanding of pitch, fine motor skills, and experimentation.

Variations: Use containers of different sizes for more notes.

3 to 4 years

Arts and Crafts Activities

Stringing Beads

Description: Offer beads and strings for preschoolers to string, creating necklaces or bracelets.

Benefits: Enhances fine motor skills, concentration, and creativity.

Variations: Use beads of different shapes and sizes.

Nature Weaving

Description: Use natural materials like twigs, leaves, and yarn to weave simple patterns or designs.

Benefits: Enhances fine motor skills, creativity, and an appreciation for nature's materials.

Variations: Experiment with different weaving patterns.

Nature Art and Sculptures

Description: Encourage preschoolers to create art and sculptures using natural materials like sticks, leaves, and stones.

Benefits: Fosters creativity, fine motor skills, and a connection to nature.

Variations: Experiment with different natural materials.

Nature Collages with Shapes

Description: Collect natural materials like leaves and create collages using predefined shapes.

Benefits: Fosters creativity, fine motor skills, and shape recognition.

Variations: Use different natural materials.

Nature Mandalas

Description: Use natural objects like flowers, leaves, and stones to create mandala designs.

Benefits: Enhances fine motor skills, creativity, and an appreciation for symmetry.

Variations: Explore different mandala patterns.

Practical Life Skills Activities

Folding Laundry

Description: Teach preschoolers to fold their own clothes, starting with simple items like washcloths and gradually progressing to larger ones.

Benefits: Enhances fine motor skills, concentration, and a sense of responsibility.

Variations: Include different types of clothing.

Simple Cooking

Description: Involve preschoolers in basic cooking tasks such as mixing, pouring, or spreading, under close supervision.

Benefits: Develops cooking skills, independence, and an understanding of food preparation.

Variations: Try age-appropriate recipes.

Planting Seeds and Garden Care

Description: Encourage preschoolers to plant seeds, care for a garden, and observe plant growth.

Benefits: Nurtures an understanding of plant biology, responsibility, and a connection to nature.

Variations: Plant different types of seeds or plants.

Sock Matching

Description: Mix up pairs of socks and have preschoolers match them by size, color, or pattern.

Benefits: Enhances fine motor skills, concentration, and the ability to recognize patterns.

Variations: Use different types of clothing items.

Table Setting for Meals

Description: Teach preschoolers how to set the table properly for meals, including arranging plates, utensils, and napkins.

Benefits: Promotes independence, responsibility, and mealtime etiquette.

Variations: Set the table for different meal types (breakfast, lunch, dinner).

Plant Care and Watering

Description: Assign preschoolers the responsibility of caring for indoor plants, including watering and observing growth.

Benefits: Nurtures a sense of responsibility, plant knowledge, and a connection to nature.

Variations: Care for different types of indoor plants.

Button Sorting

Description: Provide a variety of buttons and encourage preschoolers to sort them by size, color, or shape.

Benefits: Enhances fine motor skills, sorting abilities, and attention to detail.

Variations: Use different small objects for sorting.

Snack Preparation

Description: Involve preschoolers in making simple snacks like fruit kabobs or sandwiches with age-appropriate tasks.

Benefits: Enhances food preparation skills, independence, and an understanding of nutrition.

Variations: Experiment with different snack recipes.

Water Pouring and Transferring

Description: Provide water and small containers for preschoolers to practice pouring and transferring.

Benefits: Develops hand-eye coordination, concentration, and independence.

Variations: Use different containers and liquids.

Table Manners Practice

Description: Teach preschoolers proper table manners, including using utensils, napkin placement, and chewing with mouths closed.

Benefits: Develops etiquette, independence, and social skills.

Variations: Have a pretend tea party to practice manners.

Shoe Tying

Description: Teach preschoolers how to tie their shoes, focusing on bunny ears or other easy techniques.

Benefits: Enhances fine motor skills and independence.

Variations: Use shoes with different fastening methods.

Bed Making

Description: Show preschoolers how to make their beds neatly with proper tucking and folding.

Benefits: Promotes orderliness and responsibility.

Variations: Create a bed-making checklist.

Planting and Gardening

Description: Involve preschoolers in planting and caring for flowers or vegetables in a garden.

Benefits: Nurtures a love for nature, responsibility, and plant knowledge.

Variations: Plant different types of plants.

Cleaning Up Independently

Description: Teach preschoolers to clean up their play area and put away toys and materials.

Benefits: Promotes responsibility, orderliness, and independence.

Variations: Create a cleanup checklist.

Washing Hands Independently

Description: Teach preschoolers to wash their hands properly, emphasizing soap and water use.

Benefits: Promotes hygiene, independence, and fine motor skills.

Variations: Use different soap scents or handwashing songs.

Dressing Themselves

Description: Encourage preschoolers to dress themselves, focusing on zipping, buttoning, and putting on shoes or boots.

Benefits: Develops self-sufficiency, fine motor skills, and self-confidence.

Variations: Practice dressing for different weather conditions.

Sensory and Fine Motor Activities

Scented Sensory Bottles

Description: Together, create sensory bottles filled with scented materials like herbs, spices, or flowers for sensory exploration.

Benefits: Stimulates the sense of smell, concentration, and sensory awareness.

Variations: Use various scented materials.

Threading and Lacing Cards

Description: Provide threading cards with holes for preschoolers to practice threading and lacing with yarn or shoelaces.

Benefits: Develops fine motor skills, hand-eye coordination, and patience.

Variations: Use different threading cards.

Sensory Bins with Letters and Numbers

Description: Create sensory bins with materials like rice or beans and hide letters and numbers for recognition and counting.

Benefits: Stimulates sensory perception, letter and number recognition, and fine motor skills.

Variations: Use different sensory materials.

Playdough Creations with Patterns and Shapes

Description: Provide playdough for preschoolers to create patterns and shapes.

Benefits: Enhances fine motor skills, creativity, and mathematical thinking.

Variations: Explore different patterns and shapes.

Scented Playdough

Description: Make scented playdough using natural ingredients like herbs or flowers for sensory play.

Benefits: Stimulates the sense of smell, creativity, and fine motor skills.

Variations: Use different scents and colors.

Sensory Board

Description: Create a sensory board with various textured materials and safe interactive hardware pieces like locks, chains, gears, switches, etc.

Benefits: Develops tactile discrimination, sensory awareness, and fine motor skills.

Variations: Include different textures and materials.

Language and Communication Activities

Storytelling with Puppets and Props

Description: Encourage preschoolers to create stories using puppets and props.

Benefits: Enhances language development, storytelling skills, and creativity.

Variations: Create different puppet characters for different settings.

Letter Sound Matching Game

Description: Match objects or images with their initial letter sounds to reinforce phonics.

Benefits: Develops phonemic awareness, letter-sound association, and vocabulary.

Variations: Focus on specific letter sounds.

Nature Story Stones

Description: Paint or draw images of natural objects on stones and use them to create nature-themed stories.

Benefits: Enhances language development, storytelling skills, and creativity.

Variations: Create story stones with different themes.

Nature Alphabet Scavenger Hunt

Description: Organize scavenger hunts where preschoolers find natural objects that represent each letter of the alphabet.

Benefits: Promotes letter recognition, vocabulary, and a connection to nature.

Variations: Focus on specific letters or habitats.

Word Building with Magnetic Letters

Description: Use magnetic letters to build words and simple sentences on a magnetic board.

Benefits: Develops literacy skills, spelling, and vocabulary.

Variations: Explore different word families and sentence structures.

Picture Books and Storytelling

Description: Read picture books together and encourage preschoolers to create their own stories based on the illustrations.

Benefits: Enhances language development, storytelling skills, and creativity.

Variations: Explore books from various genres.

Math and Numeracy Activities

Counting with Natural Objects

Description: Collect natural objects like pinecones or acorns and use them for counting and math activities.

Benefits: Enhances counting skills, number recognition, and mathematical understanding.

Variations: Count different types of natural objects.

Measuring and Comparing

Description: Use simple measuring tools like rulers or tape measures to compare and measure objects.

Benefits: Introduces measurement concepts, comparison skills, and mathematical thinking.

Variations: Explore different objects and measurement units.

Money Counting and Play Store

Description: Create a play store with pretend money for preschoolers to practice counting and making purchases.

Benefits: Develops basic math skills, money awareness, and role-play abilities.

Variations: Add price tags to items or change the currency.

Nature Patterns and Geometry

Description: Explore patterns and geometry in nature by examining leaves, flowers, and natural objects.

Benefits: Enhances pattern recognition, symmetry understanding, and appreciation for natural beauty.

Variations: Collect various natural objects to study patterns.

Shape Recognition and Building

Description: Introduce geometric shapes and encourage preschoolers to build structures using these shapes.

Benefits: Enhances shape recognition, spatial skills, and creative problem-solving.

Variations: Explore different shapes and create increasingly complex structures.

Number Games and Math Puzzles

Description: Play number games and solve math puzzles that involve counting, addition, and subtraction.

Benefits: Develops numeracy skills, problem-solving abilities, and mathematical thinking.

Variations: Explore different math concepts and levels of difficulty.

Pattern Making with Colors

Description: Create patterns using colored materials like beads or buttons.

Benefits: Enhances pattern recognition, sequencing, and color awareness.

Variations: Experiment with different colors and shapes.

Science and Nature Exploration Activities

Volcano Experiment

Description: Build a volcano using paper mâché and paint, then conduct a basic volcano experiment using baking soda and vinegar to demonstrate a volcanic eruption.

Benefits: Sparks scientific curiosity, introduces basic chemical reactions, and encourages hands-on learning.

Variations: Explore different volcano shapes using different materials like sand, moss, soil or rocks.

Cloud Watching and Identification

Description: Lie on a grassy area and watch clouds, identifying different cloud types and discussing weather.

Benefits: Encourages cloud and weather observation, curiosity, and scientific interest.

Variations: Explore different cloud formations.

Seasonal Observations and Art

Description: Observe and discuss changes in the seasons and create seasonal-themed art projects.

Benefits: Teaches about the natural world, seasons, and creativity.

Variations: Explore different seasonal art techniques.

Bird Watching and Identification

Description: Set up bird feeders and watch for different bird species, identifying them using field guides.

Benefits: Fosters an appreciation for wildlife, observation skills, and an understanding of bird behavior.

Variations: Focus on specific types of birds.

Seed Germination Experiment

Description: Conduct a simple seed germination experiment to show how plants grow from seeds. Put various seeds in different wet paper tissues and observe the germination process over the next few days.

Benefits: Nurtures an understanding of plant biology and scientific curiosity.

Variations: Try different types of seeds.

Plant Life Cycle and Gardening

Description: Teach preschoolers about the life cycle of plants and involve them in gardening activities.

Benefits: Nurtures an understanding of plant biology, responsibility, and a love for gardening.

Variations: Plant different types of plants and explore various stages of the plant life cycle.

Nature Scavenger Hunt

Description: Organize nature scavenger hunts, where preschoolers search for specific natural items like pinecones or feathers.

Benefits: Fosters observation skills, connection to nature, and a sense of adventure.

Variations: Change the items to find or explore different outdoor locations.

Weather Chart and Observations

Description: Create a weather chart and have preschoolers observe and record daily weather.

Benefits: Introduces weather concepts, observation skills, and scientific exploration.

Variations: Explore different weather patterns.

Bug Hotel Creation

Description: Build a bug hotel together using natural materials like sticks, leaves, and pinecones, providing shelter for insects in your garden, promoting empathy for insects and environmental awareness.

Benefits: Nurtures empathy for insects, environmental awareness, and construction skills.

Variations: Experiment with bug hotel designs.

Geography and Cultural Activities

Around the World Cookbook

Description: Explore cuisines from different countries by cooking meals inspired by various cultures.

Benefits: Encourages cultural awareness, culinary skills, and a global perspective.

Variations: Focus on dishes from specific regions.

World Geography Puzzle

Description: Introduce preschoolers to world geography by assembling puzzles with maps of continents and countries.

Benefits: Promotes geographic awareness, problem-solving, and map-reading skills.

Variations: Use puzzles of different regions or landmarks.

Map Reading and Treasure Hunt

Description: Teach preschoolers basic map-reading skills by creating treasure maps and going on treasure hunts.

Benefits: Promotes spatial awareness, problem-solving, and a sense of adventure.

Variations: Create different treasure hunt scenarios.

Cultural Dress-Up and Celebration Day

Description: Explore cultures from around the world by dressing up in traditional clothing and exploring their cultural celebration customs through books, stories and activities.

Benefits: Encourages cultural awareness, respect for diversity, and imaginative play.

Variations: Focus on specific cultures and their attire.

Maps and Globes Exploration

Description: Introduce maps, globes, and atlases to teach basic geography concepts, including continents and countries.

Benefits: Promotes geographic awareness, map-reading skills, and global understanding.

Variations: Explore maps of different regions and continents.

Maps and Landforms

Description: Introduce maps and explore different landforms like mountains and rivers.

Benefits: Promotes geographic awareness and understanding of the world.

Variations: Explore maps of different regions.

4 to 5 years

Science and Nature Exploration Activities

Nature Scavenger Hunt

Description: Organize scavenger hunts in natural settings, encouraging children to find and identify specific objects or species.

Benefits: Stimulates observation skills, nature appreciation, and problem-solving.

Variations: Focus on different themes or ecosystems.

Solar System Exploration

Description: Learn about the solar system by creating a model, discussing planets, and exploring the concept of space.

Benefits: Fosters an interest in astronomy, scientific knowledge, and understanding of the solar system.

Variations: Explore different aspects of space.

Environmental Conservation Project

Description: Collaborate on a conservation project, such as planting trees or cleaning up a local park, discussing the importance of conservation.

Benefits: Promotes environmental awareness, a sense of responsibility, and community engagement.

Variations: Participate in different conservation projects.

Microscopic World Exploration

Description: Use microscopes to explore the microscopic world, discussing microorganisms and the importance of microscopic life.

Benefits: Enhances scientific curiosity, observation skills, and understanding of the micro world.

Variations: Explore different microscopic specimens.

Water Erosion Experiment

Description: Conduct a simple experiment to demonstrate how water erosion shapes landscapes, such as running water down a small trench in the sand on the beach.

Benefits: Sparks curiosity about geology, introduces erosion concepts, and encourages experimentation.

Variations: Experiment with different erosion scenarios.

Plant Propagation

Description: Explore plant propagation techniques, including seed sowing, cuttings, and grafting.

Benefits: Sparks curiosity about plant biology, gardening skills, and a love for greenery.

Variations: Propagate different plant species.

Physics of Flight

Description: Explore the physics of flight by creating paper airplanes, kites, and other flying objects.

Benefits: Encourages scientific curiosity, introduces physics concepts, and encourages experimentation.

Variations: Experiment with different flying designs.

Astronomy Nights

Description: Explore the night sky by observing stars, planets, and constellations during stargazing sessions.

Benefits: Fosters an interest in astronomy, scientific curiosity, and night sky awareness.

Variations: Focus on different celestial events.

Nature Classification

Description: Study classification by categorizing natural objects into groups based on specific criteria.

Benefits: Enhances classification skills, scientific thinking, and observation.

Variations: Classify different sets of natural objects.

Weather Observations

Description: Keep a weather journal, recording daily observations and discussing weather patterns.

Benefits: Encourages scientific curiosity, weather understanding, and data collection.

Variations: Track weather for different seasons.

Insect Study

Description: Explore the world of insects by observing, identifying, and learning about their habitats and behavior.

Benefits: Fosters curiosity, insect knowledge, and observation skills.

Variations: Focus on specific types of insects.

Arts and Crafts Activities

Nature Collage

Description: Gather a variety of natural materials like leaves, twigs, flowers, and pebbles. Provide children with paper and glue to create a collage using these materials.

Benefits: Encourages observation of nature, artistic expression, fine motor skills, and understanding of the environment.

Variations: Use different themes like underwater, jungle, or seasons to vary the collage materials.

Sensory Paint Exploration

Description: Prepare homemade sensory paints by mixing flour, water, and food coloring. Children can use their fingers, brushes, or sponges to paint and explore textures.

Benefits: Enhances sensory perception, creativity, fine motor skills, and color recognition.

Variations: Experiment with different textures, such as adding sand for a grainy texture or using scented paint for olfactory stimulation.

String Art

Description: Provide a piece of wood, nails, and colorful threads. Children can create geometric patterns or their own designs by wrapping the thread around the nails.

Benefits: Promotes concentration, hand-eye coordination, and geometric understanding.

Variations: Change the base material to cardboard or use different shapes like animals or letters as a base.

Seed Mosaic

Description: Offer a variety of seeds (e.g., lentils, beans, and rice) and glue. Children can create beautiful mosaic designs on cardboard using these seeds.

Benefits: Encourages fine motor skills, patience, and introduces the concept of patterns.

Variations: Use colored seeds, arrange the seeds to create specific shapes or patterns, or create a larger project over time.

Clay Sculptures

Description: Provide soft, moldable clay for sculpting. Children can use their imagination to create sculptures, animals, or abstract designs.

Benefits: Develops fine motor skills, 3D spatial awareness, and fosters creativity.

Variations: Try different types of clay, such as air-dry or polymer clay, or introduce sculpting tools for more intricate designs.

Leaf and Flower Pressing

Description: Collect leaves and flowers. Place them between sheets of paper and press them in a heavy book. After a few days, use these pressed leaves and flowers to create art.

Benefits: Teaches patience, observation, and appreciation for nature's beauty.

Variations: Experiment with different types of paper, or create greeting cards and bookmarks with the pressed materials.

Recycled Material Sculptures

Description: Collect recyclable materials like cardboard, plastic bottles, and egg cartons. Provide child-safe scissors and glue to create sculptures from these items.

Benefits: Encourages creativity, environmental awareness, and fine motor skills.

Variations: Use specific recyclable items to create a themed sculpture, such as making a robot from old boxes.

Sandpaper Art

Description: Place sandpaper beneath a piece of plain paper and let children rub crayons or pastels over it to create textured drawings.

Benefits: Enhances sensory exploration, fine motor skills, and introduces texture concepts.

Variations: Use different grades of sandpaper for varying textures or try this technique with different coloring tools like watercolors or oil pastels.

Bead Threading

Description: Provide beads and strings. Children can thread the beads to create necklaces or bracelets.

Benefits: Develops hand-eye coordination, fine motor skills, and pattern recognition.

Variations: Use different shapes and colors of beads, or introduce letter beads for spelling practice.

Torn Paper Collage

Description: Offer a variety of colored papers and encourage children to tear and glue the paper pieces to create pictures and designs.

Benefits: Enhances fine motor skills, creativity, and understanding of shapes and textures.

Variations: Experiment with different paper types, such as tissue paper, magazine cutouts, or wrapping paper.

Yarn Knitting

Description: Teach children to finger knit using yarn. They can create scarves, headbands, or simple bracelets.

Benefits: Enhances fine motor skills, hand coordination, and patience.

Variations: Experiment with different yarn types and colors, or guide children in creating more complex knitting patterns.

Leaf Rubbings

Description: Collect leaves from various trees. Place a leaf under a sheet of paper and rub a crayon over it to create leaf imprints.

Benefits: Teaches observation, fine motor skills, and introduces children to the diversity of nature.

Variations: Explore different types of leaves, create a leaf identification book, or incorporate the rubbings into larger art projects.

Shadow Art

Description: Set up a table with a strong light source and various objects like toys or figures. Children can create art by tracing the shadows of these objects on paper.

Benefits: Encourages observation, understanding of light and shadow, and creativity.

Variations: Experiment with different light angles and objects to create diverse shadow art.

Rock Painting

Description: Collect smooth, flat rocks and provide paint and brushes. Children can paint imaginative designs or creatures on the rocks.

Benefits: Enhances creativity, fine motor skills, and an appreciation for nature.

Variations: Paint rocks with themes like animals, insects, or inspirational messages. You can also varnish the rocks for a glossy finish.

Nature Dyeing

Description: Gather flowers, leaves, and berries. Children can use these natural materials to dye fabric or paper.

Benefits: Encourages an appreciation for nature, creativity, and introduces the concept of color blending.

Variations: Experiment with different fabrics and materials, or create unique designs using different combinations of natural dyes.

Sculpture Garden

Description: Provide children with clay and encourage them to sculpt small figurines. Create a miniature sculpture garden by placing these sculptures in a designated area.

Benefits: Develops fine motor skills, encourages creativity, and fosters an appreciation for art.

Variations: Consider adding natural elements like pebbles, small plants, or shells to the sculpture garden for a unique touch.

Yarn-Wrapped Letters

Description: Write letters or words on pieces of cardboard. Children can wrap colorful yarn around these letters to create textured, tactile art.

Benefits: Enhances fine motor skills, letter recognition, and introduces early literacy concepts.

Variations: Customize this activity based on the child's name or favorite words. Experiment with different colors and types of yarn.

Homemade Musical Instruments

Description: Encourage children to make simple musical instruments like shakers using empty containers and dried beans, or drums using empty coffee cans.

Benefits: Fosters creativity, rhythm, and an understanding of sound and music.

Variations: Experiment with different materials and sizes to create a variety of homemade instruments, such as tambourines or rainsticks.

Patterned Nature Prints

Description: Collect leaves, flowers, and other natural materials. Children can dip these items in paint and create patterned prints on paper or fabric.

Benefits: Encourages an appreciation for nature, introduces patterns, and fosters creativity.

Variations: Use different colored paints or experiment with various printing surfaces like canvas or fabric.

Fruit and Vegetable Stamps

Description: Cut fruits and vegetables like apples, potatoes, and celery in half. Dip these in paint and use them as stamps to create artwork.

Benefits: Introduces different textures and shapes, enhances creativity, and teaches about fruits and vegetables.

Variations: Try different fruits and vegetables to create diverse stamp patterns and artwork.

Origami

Description: Provide children with square pieces of paper and teach them simple origami folds to create various paper animals, flowers, or shapes.

Benefits: Enhances fine motor skills, patience, and introduces geometry concepts.

Variations: Start with basic origami designs and gradually progress to more complex ones as children become more skilled.

Collaborative Mural Painting

Description: Provide a large sheet of paper or cardboard and let children collaborate on a mural by painting together.

Benefits: Fosters teamwork, creativity, and allows children to express themselves in a group project.

Variations: Theme the mural based on children's interests or the season, or use various painting techniques like finger painting or splatter painting.

Practical Life Skills Activities

Basic Electrical Knowledge

Description: Introduce children to basic electrical knowledge, teaching them about electrical outlets, plugs, and safety.

Benefits: Promotes safety awareness, practical skills, and understanding of electricity.

Variations: Explore different electrical appliances.

Basic Car Maintenance

Description: Teach children basic car maintenance skills, such as checking tire pressure and oil levels.

Benefits: Promotes safety, practical skills, and understanding of vehicle maintenance.

Variations: Explore different aspects of car care.

Planting and Harvesting

Description: Continue exploring gardening by involving children in the planting and harvesting of vegetables or fruits.

Benefits: Nurtures an understanding of food production, responsibility, and sustainability.

Variations: Grow different types of crops.

Basic First Aid

Description: Teach children basic first-aid skills like applying band-aids, cleaning and disinfecting minor cuts and scrapes.

Benefits: Promotes safety, self-reliance, and preparedness in emergencies.

Variations: Practice different first-aid techniques.

Organizing a Closet

Description: Involve children in organizing their own closet, arranging clothes by type, season, or color.

Benefits: Develops organization skills, independence, and a sense of order.

Variations: Organize different sections of the closet.

Basic Woodworking

Description: Introduce children to basic woodworking with age-appropriate tools to create simple wooden projects.

Benefits: Fosters craftsmanship, fine motor skills, and creativity.

Variations: Explore different woodworking projects.

Basic Sewing

Description: Teach children basic sewing skills using child-safe needles, fabric, and simple stitching techniques.

Benefits: Enhances fine motor skills, patience, and introduces a practical skill.

Variations: Create simple sewing projects like a felt ornament.

Shoe Tying

Description: Teach preschoolers how to tie their shoes, starting with simple knots and progressing to shoelaces.

Benefits: Enhances fine motor skills, independence, and self-care abilities.

Variations: Practice with different types of shoelaces.

Cooking Meals

Description: Involve preschoolers in more complex cooking tasks, such as measuring ingredients and following recipes.

Benefits: Develops cooking skills, math concepts, and an appreciation for food preparation.

Variations: Explore diverse cuisines and dishes.

Self-Setting Table

Description: Teach preschoolers to set the table independently, including arranging plates, utensils, and cups.

Benefits: Promotes independence, fine motor skills, and mealtime etiquette.

Variations: Set the table for different meals or occasions.

Dishwashing

Description: Involve preschoolers in washing dishes, starting with non-breakable items and gradually progressing to more delicate ones.

Benefits: Develops responsibility, hand-eye coordination, and practical life skills.

Variations: Use different types of dishes and utensils.

Plant Care and Gardening

Description: Assign preschoolers the responsibility of caring for a garden, including planting, weeding, and harvesting.

Benefits: Nurtures an understanding of plant biology, responsibility, and a connection to nature.

Variations: Plant different types of vegetables or flowers.

Sensory and Fine Motor Activities

Building with Blocks

Description: Encourage children to build structures using wooden blocks, promoting creativity and problem-solving.

Benefits: Enhances spatial awareness, fine motor skills, and imaginative play.

Variations: Build different types of structures.

Aromatherapy with Herbs

Description: Explore aromatherapy by drying and using herbs to create scented sachets or potpourri.

Benefits: Enhances sensory perception, relaxation, and an understanding of scents.

Variations: Experiment with different herbs and scents.

Nature Photography

Description: Introduce children to photography by allowing them to take pictures of the natural world and discussing their observations.

Benefits: Develops observation skills, creativity, and an appreciation for photography.

Variations: Explore different photography themes.

Texture Exploration Book

Description: Create a tactile exploration book with pages featuring various textures for children to touch and describe.

Benefits: Enhances sensory perception, vocabulary, and fine motor skills.

Variations: Include different textures and materials.

String Art

Description: Explore string art by using pins, strings, and a corkboard to create geometric patterns or images.

Benefits: Fosters creativity, fine motor skills, and an understanding of geometry.

Variations: Experiment with different designs and colors.

Pottery and Clay Sculpting

Description: Introduce pottery and clay sculpting, allowing children to create three-dimensional art.

Benefits: Fosters creativity, fine motor skills, and an understanding of sculptural art.

Variations: Experiment with different clay types and techniques.

Nature Weaving

Description: Use natural materials like long grasses or twigs to create simple weaving projects.

Benefits: Enhances fine motor skills, creativity, and an appreciation for natural materials.

Variations: Explore different weaving patterns.

Nature Art with Found Objects

Description: Use natural objects like sticks, leaves, and stones to create sculptures or collages.

Benefits: Enhances creativity, fine motor skills, and an appreciation for nature's materials.

Variations: Explore different art forms and themes.

Threading and Beading

Description: Provide beads and strings for preschoolers to thread and create jewelry or patterns.

Benefits: Enhances fine motor skills, concentration, and creativity.

Variations: Use beads of different shapes and materials.

Language and Communication Activities

Mime Time

Description: Fill a bowl with names of animals, characters or people on pieces of paper and take turns at picking a name and trying to make the other person guess the animal by imitating in silence.

Benefits: Enhances creativity, problem-solving and teamwork.

Variations: Use a hourglass and guess as many animals, characters or people as possible within a certain timeframe.

Nature-inspired Storytelling

Description: Encourage children to create stories inspired by nature, using elements like animals, trees, and landscapes.

Benefits: Enhances storytelling skills, language development, and imagination.

Variations: Explore different natural themes.

Bilingual Learning

Description: Introduce children to a new language, promoting bilingualism through songs, stories, and basic conversations.

Benefits: Enhances language development, cognitive skills, and cultural awareness.

Variations: Explore different languages.

Creative Storytelling

Description: Encourage children to create and illustrate their own stories, fostering storytelling skills and artistic expression.

Benefits: Enhances narrative abilities, creativity, and fine motor skills.

Variations: Explore different story genres.

Storytelling with Puppets

Description: Encourage preschoolers to create and perform puppet shows, developing storytelling skills and creativity.

Benefits: Enhances language development, imagination, and dramatic play.

Variations: Create puppet characters for different stories.

Reading Comprehension

Description: Read age-appropriate books and engage preschoolers in discussions about the story, characters, and lessons.

Benefits: Enhances comprehension skills, vocabulary, and critical thinking.

Variations: Explore books from different genres and cultures.

Math and Numeracy Activities

Nature-inspired Geometry

Description: Explore geometry concepts using natural objects, discussing shapes, angles, and symmetry.

Benefits: Develops geometry understanding, math skills, and observation.

Variations: Explore different geometric concepts.

Fraction Exploration

Description: Introduce children to fractions using natural objects like fruits or shapes to illustrate fractions.

Benefits: Develops understanding of fractions, math skills, and problem-solving.

Variations: Explore different fractions.

Money Math Challenges

Description: Create money-related math challenges where children solve problems involving addition, subtraction, and money calculations.

Benefits: Develops financial literacy, math skills, and problem-solving.

Variations: Explore different math challenges.

Time-telling with Sundials

Description: Learn about time-telling by creating and using simple sundials in an outdoor setting.

Benefits: Promotes time awareness, an understanding of sundials, and observational skills.

Variations: Explore sundials in different locations.

Math Story Problems

Description: Create math story problems based on real-life situations and encourage children to solve them.

Benefits: Develops math skills, problem-solving abilities, and mathematical reasoning.

Variations: Explore different math concepts.

Calendar Math

Description: Engage in calendar-related math activities, such as calculating days between dates or identifying patterns.

Benefits: Enhances calendar skills, math concepts, and logical thinking.

Variations: Create calendar-based challenges.

Money Management

Description: Introduce children to basic money management, including saving, spending, and budgeting for small expenses.

Benefits: Develops financial literacy, math skills, and responsibility.

Variations: Explore different financial scenarios.

Calendar Activities

Description: Teach children about calendars, days of the week, months, and special events through calendar-related activities like a DIY chocolate Advent calendar.

Benefits: Promotes time awareness, calendar skills, and organization.

Variations: Create themed calendars.

Counting Collections

Description: Collect objects from nature like leaves or rocks and practice counting and grouping them.

Benefits: Develops counting skills, number recognition, and basic math concepts.

Variations: Count different types of natural objects.

Shape Scavenger Hunt

Description: Organize shape-themed scavenger hunts in nature, searching for objects that match specific shapes.

Benefits: Enhances shape recognition, geometry understanding, and observation skills.

Variations: Focus on different shapes.

Geography and Cultural Activities

Mapping Adventures

Description: Go on mapping adventures where children use maps to navigate and explore different locations.

Benefits: Promotes map-reading skills, geographic awareness, and exploration.

Variations: Explore different maps and destinations.

World Flags

Description: Learn about flags from around the world, discussing their symbolism and the countries they represent.

Benefits: Encourages cultural awareness, flag recognition, and a global perspective.

Variations: Explore flags from different continents.

Cultural Cooking Experiments

Description: Conduct cooking experiments by recreating traditional dishes from different cultures, discussing their ingredients and history.

Benefits: Encourages cultural appreciation, culinary skills, and global awareness.

Variations: Explore dishes from specific countries.

World Geography Board Game

Description: Play a geography-themed board game that explores world countries, landmarks, and cultural facts.

Benefits: Promotes geographic awareness, critical thinking, and global knowledge.

Variations: Try different geography board games.

Cultural Festivals

Description: Explore cultural festivals from around the world, discussing their traditions, music, food, and celebrations.

Benefits: Encourages cultural appreciation, global awareness, and a sense of celebration.

Variations: Explore festivals from different Continents

Puzzle Map

Description: Learn about continents by using puzzle maps to identify and place continents in their correct locations.

Benefits: Promotes geographic awareness, spatial understanding, and world geography.

Variations: Explore different aspects of continents.

Cultural Dance Exploration

Description: Explore traditional dances from different cultures, allowing children to learn and perform them.

Benefits: Encourages cultural appreciation, physical coordination, and an understanding of dance.

Variations: Explore dances from specific cultures.

Landform Models

Description: Create 3D models of geographic landforms like mountains, valleys, and rivers using craft materials.

Benefits: Promotes geographic awareness, spatial understanding, and creativity.

Variations: Explore different landforms.

Social and Emotional Development Activities

Feelings Charades

Description: Children act out different emotions (e.g., happy, sad, angry) without using words. Others guess the emotion being portrayed.

Benefits: Enhances emotional recognition and expression, fosters empathy, and improves communication skills.

Variations: Use picture cards with various emotional expressions, or act out scenarios that trigger different emotions.

Emotion Stones

Description: Paint various emotions (happy, sad, surprised, etc.) on stones. Children can pick a stone and share a time when they felt that emotion.

Benefits: Promotes emotional self-awareness, encourages open communication, and helps children understand that it's okay to feel different emotions.

Variations: Add more nuanced emotions or combine emotions on a single stone (e.g., happy and surprised).

Emotion Cards and Stories

Description: Create emotion cards with facial expressions. Read stories or scenarios, and ask children to match the emotion card to how the character might be feeling.

Benefits: Enhances emotional vocabulary, empathy, and understanding of others' feelings.

Variations: Use real-life photos or illustrations on the cards to depict different emotions.

Gratitude Journal

Description: Provide children with a journal to write or draw something they are thankful for each day.

Benefits: Promotes a positive outlook, self-reflection, and gratitude, which can lead to emotional well-being.

Variations: Encourage children to create a "happiness jar" where they write down daily moments of joy to read later.

Feelings Check-In Circle

Description: Gather in a circle and ask children to share how they're feeling today. Discuss reasons for those emotions in a safe and supportive environment.

Benefits: Encourages emotional expression, active listening, and empathetic responses.

Variations: Use a "feeling wheel" with various emotional words to help children describe their emotions more precisely.

Emotion Masks

Description: Provide blank masks or templates for children to decorate as they feel at the moment. Discuss why they chose specific expressions.

Benefits: Encourages creativity, emotional expression, and self-awareness.

Variations: Use different materials like paper plates or craft foam for the masks, or provide props that represent emotions.

Gratitude Circle

Description: Sit in a circle and have each child express something they are thankful for. Encourage them to think about everyday things that bring joy.

Benefits: Promotes gratitude, mindfulness, and positive thinking.

Variations: Create a gratitude tree by drawing or placing leaves on a tree with what each child is thankful for.

Mindfulness and Breathing Exercises

Description: Teach children simple mindfulness techniques like deep breathing or guided imagery to help them manage their emotions.

Benefits: Enhances emotional regulation, reduces stress, and improves self-awareness.

Variations: Incorporate movement with mindfulness exercises, such as yoga for kids.

REFERENCES

Anthony, D. (2023, April 21). *Famous Montessori student success stories*. Primary Montessori. https://primarymontessori.com/famous-montessori-student-success-stories/

Burnett, C. (2020, May 17). *Rainbow magic milk science experiment*. Childhood101. https://childhood101.com/magic-milk-science-experiment/

The environment: Materials. (n.d.).Virtual Lab School. https://www.virtuallabschool.org/infant-toddler/learning-environments/lesson-4

Eva. (2020, April 23). *7 classic baking soda and vinegar activities to do with your kids*. KidMinds. https://kidminds.org/classic-baking-soda-and-vinegar-activities/

How We Montessori. (2023, July 7). *Creating a Montessori bedroom for your two-year-old*. Lovevery. https://lovevery.com/community/blog/child-development/how-to-montessori-your-two-year-olds-bedroom-by-howwemontessori/

Isaacs, B. (n.d.). *The Montessori method: Encouraging independence*. Teach Early Years. https://www.teachearlyyears.com/learning-and-development/view/the-montessori-method-encouraging-independence

Jones, S. (2022, October 4). *How is science taught in Montessori?* Montessori for Today. https://montessorifortoday.com/how-is-science-taught-in-montessori/

Juju. (2023, July 6). *How to recognise and support sensitive periods in your child's development.* Montessori Academy. https://montessoriacademy.com.au/how-to-recognise-and-support-sensitive-periods-in-your-childs-development/

Ledendecker, M. (2019, December 23). *Seven little ways to create a Montessori home environment.* The Montessori School of the Berkshires. https://www.berkshiremontessori.org/msb-blog/7ways-montessori-home-environment

Montessori, M. (n.d.). *Maria Montessori quotes.* Montessori 150. https://montessori150.org/maria-montessori/montessori-quotes/

Success stories. (n.d.). Living Montessori Education Community. https://www.livingmontessori.com/our-school/success-stories/

Made in the USA
Las Vegas, NV
27 December 2024